Michael Evamy

Laurence
King
Publishing

LAURENCE KING

First published in 2007

This mini edition published in 2015 by
Laurence King Publishing Ltd
361–373 City Road
London EC1V 1LR
United Kingdom

Tel: +44 20 7841 6900
Fax: +44 20 7841 6910

e-mail: enquiries@laurenceking.com
www.laurenceking.com

A catalogue record for this book is
available from the British Library.

ISBN 978 1 78067 180 2

Printed in China

Designed by Spin

Cover designed by Pentagram

What is in this book?

In this book you will find many of the greatest logos ever designed: some that have been widely acknowledged as such and others that will be. There is work by masters of symbol and logotype design, such as Paul Rand, Saul Bass, Otl Aicher, Anton Stankowski and Lance Wyman, alongside marks by today's big names and emerging talents, including North, Sagmeister Inc, Open, Spin, Johnson Banks, Browns and Segura Inc. In all, 'Logo' contains work submitted by more than 150 leading design firms of all sizes, from across Europe, North America and the Far East, plus dozens of outstanding identities, mostly of a certain vintage, sourced from the client companies themselves. All the logos that have been included were in use at the time that the book was originally researched.

This book is about what we see around us now, regardless of when it was designed. It contains logos that date back over a century and a handful that were still to be launched when this book was written and designed. Our aim, above all, has been to provide a true, broad and unique reflection of the state of the art in high quality corporate identity design in the early twenty-first century.

The book has been designed by Spin, the London-based creators of identities for Channel Five, the Whitechapel Gallery and the Institute of Contemporary Arts. Logos are almost exclusively displayed in black and white or greyscale to better highlight the formal qualities of each logo, which are detracted from when several marks appear in full colour on a single page, leading to a Times Square effect of logos clamouring for attention.

How are logos arranged?

Marks have been categorized according to their most significant visual features or characteristics, for example, overlapping type, square symbols, symbols containing trees. To create a sense of the impulses and trends currently at play in identity design, the material was given the chance to order itself; groups of logos were allowed to coalesce naturally into categories. Some did this more naturally than others. Also, there were many instances in which a logo could have legitimately been placed in any of three or four categories. So a few designs may not be exactly where you might expect.

There are three sections: one on text-based logos (Logotypes and letters), one on pictorial and abstract emblems (Symbols) and a final, brief section on logo systems (Families and sequences).

There are also 40 'focus' logos: identities that have either been outstandingly influential or are outstandingly good, and which have been given their own page and extended caption.

Captions and credits
The caption for each logo identifies the organization and its area of activity, the country of its headquarters, the designer or design firm responsible and the date of design. Many of the logos need no further explanation, but extra insights and stories about designs have been provided wherever possible.

Credits for individuals have been included in captions where requested by design firms. Positions and roles on projects have been abbreviated according to information provided (bearing in mind that similar functions are known by a variety of names in the design industry):

    AD: art director(s)
    CD: creative director(s)
    DD: design director(s)
    SD: senior designer(s)
    D: designer(s)

Two design firms featured share the name Coast Design, one based in Brussels, one in Sydney. In captions, the former is referred to as 'Coast' and the latter as 'Coast Design (Sydney)'.

Acknowledgments
To all of the individuals at companies that submitted work and helped to keep the quality high, a big thank you. There are too many to mention by name but there are several whose time and care I especially appreciate, namely: Steff Geissbuhler at C&G Partners, Lance Wyman, Simon Beresford-Smith at Pentagram and Laura Roche at FutureBrand.

Thanks also to Jo Lightfoot at Laurence King, who gave me the opportunity to do this book; to the book's editor Catherine Hooper for her air of calm and superior grasp of written English; to Ian Macfarlane and Chris Allen at Spin for their design genius and sensitivity to the material; and to Angelina Li for chasing companies with tireless charm.

Thanks to Browns, Atelier Works, Thomas Manss, SEA and Untitled for repeatedly putting their faith in me as a copywriter and for making the experience of working with them so enjoyable and enlightening.

Lastly but mostly, my thanks and love go to my wife, Samantha, and our two young sons, Lucas and Thomas, who have all contributed ideas, patience and perseverance beyond the call of duty. Finally, an apology: to Lucas, for not finding a place for the logos of Superman, The Fantastic Four and X-Men. Bad, bad Dad.

7 What is a logo?

8 Where do logos come from?

10 Who makes logos?

12 Can logos change anything? And why do logos get changed?

14 What do logos mean?

16 Where do logos go?

The logo is the focal point of any identity system and the key to its acceptance.

What is a logo?

Logos are signs, marks of identity designed for easy recognition. They are used by every kind of organization in every part of the world, from international corporations to charities and from political parties to community groups and schools. Logos also identify individual products and services.

Most people think of logos only as symbols containing some kind of abstract or pictorial element, in the manner of Nike's 'swoosh' or WWF's panda. But a logo can equally be just a combination of typographic elements – letters, words, numerals and punctuation marks – set in a chosen typeface, such as the 3M and Kellogg's logos. In fact, a logotype, the word from which we get 'logo', is exactly that: a single piece of type. Most of the time, logos operate on a sliding scale between the purely verbal and the purely visual: a word with a letter that makes a visual pun, for example, or a symbol containing a company name.

Logos or 'brand identities' (as created by these companies) are usually one small part of a far bigger identity package, which can include a new name and slogan, the development of a 'brand architecture' and numerous applications of a corporate visual system and verbal 'tone of voice'. However, the fact remains that the logo is the focal point of any identity system and the key to its acceptance. Designing logos is generally seen as the quintessential graphic designer's art. It is the compression of meaning into just a few memorable marks, the distillation of the big and complex into something simple and unique that presents one of the defining design challenges of the modern era. No other part of a graphic design firm's output will be on such public display or be open to such intense scrutiny. As a communicator, there is no better way of making your mark on the world.

The ubiquity of logos, and their great power to unlock memories, feelings and associations, are the product of 150 years of exponential growth in the field of advertising and corporate communications.

Kellogg's ®

Where do logos come from?

Logos – or their equivalents – are as old as civilization itself. It is widely considered that branding, as a means of identifying an object's ownership, has its roots in the marking of cattle hides and horns by large estates and temples in Ancient Egypt, and in the development by Greek and Roman craftsmen of 'maker's marks', which allowed goods to be traded with confidence anywhere across an entire empire, regardless of their place of origin. This is continued in the role of trademarks today.

In medieval Europe, heraldry was conceived as a means of recognizing helmeted friends and foes on the battlefield. Crosses, crescents, animals, mythical creatures and flowers abounded. The concept of verbal identity also arrived in the form of mottoes. Simultaneously, cattle branding became standard practice in Mexico, thanks to Christopher Columbus, and was later developed by Texas ranchers as a deterrent to rustlers. They fashioned branding irons into combinations of shapes, letters and symbols that would be hard for poachers to turn into their own marks.

Branding continues to this day, and not just of livestock. Human branding also has a history, through the slave trade, Tsarist Russia, Nazi Germany and, today, in tattoo parlours and American university fraternities.

However, the Bible tells of an instance of branding that pre-dates just about everything. The world's first logo was, it seems, God's work. The Old Testament reports that God 'put a mark on Cain'. This was meant not as a punishment for killing his brother – why simply mark someone when you could just as easily smite them with boils? – but as a means of protection from others who might have wanted to take the law into their own hands. The mark was God's 'keep off' sign, addressed to potential Edenite vigilante groups.

We can only speculate as to what kind of visual device the Almighty would have employed to convey his key marketing message in an instantly understandable and persuasive way to the target audience – the skill that is the holy grail for all aspiring logo designers. God being God, he would have found a way. And, by all accounts, it worked: Cain led an

untroubled life, moving to Nod, east of Eden, and raising not just a family but also an entire city. Indeed, the almost unbounded good fortune of his new life could have owed a great deal to his exclusive right to bear the God brand.

Today, the world's omnipotent brands belong not to deities but to fast-food groups, drinks manufacturers, banks, telecoms giants and airlines. The ubiquity of their logos, and their great power to unlock memories, feelings and associations, are the product of 150 years of exponential growth in the field of advertising and corporate communications.

In the nineteenth century, the packaging of early mass-produced goods was branded with company insignia to aid their distribution from centralized factories and to differentiate them from locally produced competitor products. In the USA, to engender trust in the new non-local products, companies such as Kellogg's and Campbell's employed the signature of their founder, while elsewhere human emblems were used, such as the rosy-cheeked quaker of Quaker Oats and the African-American Uncle Ben (a Texas rice-grower) and Aunt Jemima (a baker of pancakes for her white master and his guests).

In the UK, the 1875 Trademarks Registration Act came into effect on 1 January 1876. That morning a nameless employee of Bass & Co, the Burton on Trent-based brewery, having spent the night outside the registrar's office, was the first to register the trademark for the company's pale ale: a simple red triangle, conceived successfully to provide instant recognition on a barrel or bottle. The emblem – now with three-dimensional edges – continues to appear on bottles and cans.

Other long-lasting logos originating from this time include those of Shell, Mercedes-Benz, Ford and Michelin. But it was a German business that pioneered what is now called corporate identity. In 1906, the electrical goods group AEG hired an 'artistic advisor', Peter Behrens, who was given the brief of transforming and unifying the image of the sprawling company. It was the first appointment of its kind. Behrens, a trained architect, was given licence to design new buildings, products and graphic material. The AEG logo he designed in 1912 is still in use, unchanged in almost a century.

But the real age of the logo arrived after World War II, when booming demand for goods in the USA, stoked by the new medium of television advertising, unleashed a flood of new products and businesses. The growth in department stores and supermarkets meant that packaging had to work ten times as hard to catch the shopper's eye. Logos and graphics that were visually simple and immediate won attention; applied consistently and repetitively across packaging and advertising, they won loyalty.

In logo design, Paul Rand was the master. Rand took the modern Swiss approach of stern graphic simplicity and sans-serif fonts, and gave it a smile. Rand had the knack of giving faceless corporations a personality, often by reducing their existing logos to simple humanistic

elements, and then carrying the clarity and personality through to packaging, annual reports and other material. He added a package with a bow to the shield of United Parcel Service (UPS); he turned the antique 'W' of Westinghouse into what looked like a cartoon crown; and he lightened and harmonized the logo for computer giant IBM by 'striping' the thick heavy letterforms. Rand's model of making the simple memorable and timeless gave all future logo designers a yardstick with which to measure their efforts.

In the meantime, agencies such as Walter Landor & Associates (now Landor & Associates) in San Francisco and Lippincott Margulies (now Lippincott Mercer) in Manhattan grew quickly on the back of packaging design programmes and logo creation and then entrenched themselves in the emerging field of corporate identity, helping corporations to build brand awareness at home and abroad. In 1960s London, new agencies like Pentagram, Minale Tattersfield and Wolff Olins followed suit, the latter reintroducing pictorial symbols to mainstream identity design, with a fox for Hadfields, the paint manufacturer, in 1967 and a hummingbird for Bovis, the construction company, in 1971.

A logo is useful as an identifier and as a point of difference. Symbols, in particular, could be understood by people of different languages and cultures within large cities or in countries beyond the logo's place of origin. However, as companies grew and diversified across industrial, commercial and national boundaries, the scope of identity programmes also expanded. From logos and packaging, identity systems came to encompass a welter of media and environments as the biggest brands sought to exert a greater hold on consumer behaviour. Coordinated advertising and sponsorship campaigns, branded packaging, printed literature, retail fit-outs and point-of-sale displays all helped to boost 'brand awareness' (not the same as brand popularity). The identity industry boomed and fragmented.

Since the 1980s, waves of globalization, deregulation, consolidation, restructuring and repositioning, accompanied by the revolution of electronic communication, have presented new challenges and opportunities to the managers of corporate and brand identity. The steeply rising processing power of computers and other new media have enabled new images and new complexity to be built into visual identities.

Despite all of the investment in brand 'experience', digital marketing and 'holistic brand relationship' creation, the logo continues to provide the kernel of any identity programme. Logos seem to offer the most concise available visual index of graphic design; evidence of the factors that change the practice of design – emerging styles and attitudes, new technology, the Internet – is seen first and by the widest audience in logos.

There are more organizations, products and services competing for more of our attention than ever before. Very rapidly, the man, woman and child in the street have become adept at interpreting the signs of identity and ownership around them. Today, everyone has a point of view about the latest logo. It seems to be a natural human impulse to seek out meanings in them – meanings that experts in branding and corporate identity frequently seem unable to anticipate.

Gone are the days when company bosses plucked idiosyncratic corporate symbols from the ether.

Who makes logos?

THE
ROYAL
PARKS

Broadly, logos are commissioned by marketing departments or other individuals within an organization and created either by in-house graphic designers or by an external design agency. Approval for a design usually has to be sought from the senior management of the organization and, in some cases, may lie solely with its head. The process of approving and finalizing a logo can take months and can erode a design's quality and distinctiveness. Moon's logo for The Royal Parks, on the other hand, was unexpectedly given the thumbs up by HM The Queen within 24 hours.

For most organizations, the visual identity overhaul that ensues from a change of logo usually means a major investment. The process involves a number of stages, including a research phase to assess the client's current identity and market position, to identify its ambitions and to establish an intellectual platform for the design (and, possibly, naming) phase. Then there is the design of the identity and all of the material it is applied to. This can involve other specialist skills. Dalton Maag, the London-based typographic consultancy, offers a 'logo refinement' service that exhaustively tests and hones a logo's lettering and spacing for optimum legibility, whether it is just a few pixels in height or blazed across a billboard.

For major businesses, the total bill can easily run into many millions, after fees for research, branding advice, design, internal communications and training, a launch event, press, PR, advertising and further research. There is also the cost of rebranding premises, vehicles and products and the production of new stationery, literature, websites, and so on. All of which militates against risk-taking and originality. Gone are the days when company bosses plucked idiosyncratic corporate symbols from the ether, such as Goodyear's winged boot, inspired by a statuette of the Roman god Mercury in the home of founder Frank Seiberling. Now, there are tiers of management and marketing all erring on the side of safety and trusting in reams of customer research.

At the other end of the cost scale, there are companies in the mould of Logoworks, an online ordering service that offers clients a range of logo design packages and 'initial logo concepts...in just 3 business days'. Logoworks employs more than 200 designers and had sales of $7.3 million in 2005. In 2006, it was the 66th fastest growing business in the USA, according to the Inc. 500 rankings. For small to mid-sized American businesses, Logoworks and the like are answering a call for inexpensive, badge-like identities and a design process unburdened by intellectual enquiry or deliberation. Co-founder Morgan Lynch laid bare his insecurities about professional design consultancy to 'Inc.' magazine when talking about his earlier experience in a software start-up that went to a local agency for an identity. 'Eventually we got a logo that was okay, but I didn't like paying bills for people thinking about our stuff. The design process seemed flawed.'

A logo is like a lens that an organization holds up to itself.

Can logos change anything?
And why do logos get changed?

<u>Corporate logos help us to distinguish one organization from another. The way a logo does this is by reflecting, visually, the activities, values or attributes that represent the organization best – in the view of the organization's leaders.</u>

A logo can create expectations of, say, a new business or service, but on its own it cannot change opinions that have already been formed through personal encounters with the business. It is the experience of individuals that gives a logo real associations and real meaning.

Put another way, a logo is like a lens that an organization holds up to itself. If there is light behind the lens in the form of outstanding products, a memorable customer experience and excellent supplier relationships, it will shine; the logo will offer a piercing beam of positive associations. If there is no light, there is nothing to see, and swapping lenses will not make a blind bit of difference.

If a struggling business changes its logo and nothing else, it will continue to flounder. Successful new logos signify positive change within organizations. The success of the Tate logo in the UK is down to its accurate portrayal of the modernization and realignment of the four Tate galleries, which have dramatically enhanced the visitor experience. To view it only as a nice bit of type is to stunt its achievement.

A logo change can signal a shift in management direction or a revitalization of corporate culture or values. A typical example is BT, which claimed in 2003 that its newly launched globe of many colours 'reflects the wide range of activities that BT now encompasses'. There can be little argument that the new logo is better suited to this role than the previous 'piper' emblem.

There are plenty of other reasons for an identity change or update, a change in name being an obvious one. It may be that a company has outgrown its logo – the design has become misleading about the company's range of activities or simply looks dated. Intricate older logos can fail to reproduce well, especially in electronic media. Or there may be a legal need to change a symbol.

A change of identity is occasionally part of a larger campaign to shed an unhealthy reputation. Philip Morris Companies renamed itself Altria Group in 2003, adopted an abstract mark of a grid of richly coloured squares and set off on a public relations and philanthropic charm offensive, none of which was able to disguise the fact that its products could kill.

Symbols that become controversial may need to be shuffled offstage. Robertson's, makers of jams and marmalades, introduced its 'Golly' mark in 1910 after the son of the founder noticed children in rural America playing with black rag dolls made from their mothers' discarded clothes. In 2002 after sustained pressure from groups that considered the mascot racist, it was pensioned off. The company insisted its withdrawal had nothing to do with political correctness, attributing it instead to the character's dwindling popularity with children. Another notorious example is British Airways' U-turn on its 'ethnic' tailfins, after former prime minister Margaret Thatcher draped her handkerchief over the rear of a model 747 to register her disapproval.

It is always tempting to ditch an identity when times are tough but it is never an answer in itself. Few are the businesses with the confidence to stick by their logo through thick and thin. A notable exception is Apple, whose rise and rise back to success began with the iMac and continued with the iPod and iTunes. Its logo was not looking quite so tempting or iconic, though, in the mid-1990s when the company was still churning out beige boxes and chancing its arm on concepts such as the Apple Newton. As the father of modern logo design Paul Rand has often been quoted as saying, the Chanel logo 'only smells as good as the perfume it stands for'.

Does this mean that it doesn't matter what a logo looks like as long as it functions as a sign? Pretty much. However, the best signs are highly visible, communicating quickly and clearly. And clarity, especially in today's business environment, is not easy to achieve. Also, logos are not like traffic signs; they do not belong to a system of similar logos. Each one must be unique or, better still, memorable if it is to work as a mark of identity. Furthermore, if it is to have any kind of shelf-life, it must resist design fads and fashions. All of this takes a lot of design.

Meaning is of little importance compared to the associations that customers make with organizations as a result of their own dealings with them.

Swiss Re

What do logos mean?

<u>Logos do not have to mean anything. Their main purpose is to be informative: to convey to whom or what something, someone or somewhere belongs.</u>

Just because a logo doesn't have to mean anything doesn't mean it can't. A logo's effectiveness as a mark of identity lies in its degree of difference. To make logos unique, designers apply the visual tools at their disposal – typography, form, colour – and draw on the points of difference that distinguish an organization's individual culture, ethos, activities and mission. They can add meaning to logos, although that meaning is of little importance compared to the associations that customers make with organizations as a result of their own dealings with them.

To read more into a logo, you need to look at the choice of typeface, its weight, the character spacing, the relative position of words and the content and visual style of the symbolic elements. Typefaces, like people, possess distinct personalities – contemporary, traditional, stark,

reserved, extrovert, decorative, impulsive – that can quickly convey the nature of an organization.

The logo for Barneys New York, designed in 1981 by Steff Geissbuhler when he was at Chermayeff & Geismar Inc., is simply two levels of statuesque, extravagantly spaced capital letters, capturing perfectly the image of one of the world's most stylish and exclusive fashion outlets. Such details as unconventional ligatures, punctuation marks and the arrangement of a logo's elements can impart other information or simply entertain. At the heart of the Barneys logo, for instance, the position of the 'N' over the 'Y' of New York underlines the store's pride in its location.

Some logos need no explanation. If the symbolism is obvious or its connection with the organization is clear, then everyone understands. Others employ symbols that seem to have a negligible connection with their organization's activity, and it hasn't done Apple, Lacoste, Kipling, Godiva, Starbucks, Shell, Mercedes and a host of other big brands any harm.

However, we do, as a species, feel the need to seek meaning in images. We like stories, and pictorial logos can provide that kind of fixed narrative. It is when presented with more abstract logos that our minds head off down different avenues. In an article in 'Eye' in 1998, Will Novosedelik reported the ways in which a conference audience (not of customers, but marketing professionals) in Phoenix interpreted the new identity for Lucent Technologies. It was presented to them by a director of Landor, whose work it was, yet the connection with the concept of light, from the Latin word 'lux', passed much of the audience by. Instead, links were made with Lucifer, which led to the accompanying symbol – a hand-painted scarlet circle – taking on, in the audience's eyes, an air of diabolical menace.

Non-objective logos were originally intended to act simply as signs without specific meaning, to which we attach our own associations. But human nature demands more. Which is why businesses of a more controlling nature – or their consultants

– are now in the habit of issuing lengthy, pseudish rationalizations of their new logos' symbolism. These earnest ramblings are intended to guide us towards the designated interpretation. They tend not to see the light of day in the press and that is possibly just as well for the credibility of the companies concerned. They could be interpreted as a way of justifying the high cost of a project to shareholders: 'Yes, it was expensive...but look at how much symbolism we got!'

For example, when Interbrand produced a three-dimensional 'evolution' of the classic AT&T logo by Saul Bass, it claimed the following: 'A new luminosity makes the brand more approachable and a degree of transparency helps capture the honesty and openness central to the revitalized brand.' Mastercard, in introducing its new identity in June 2006 stated: 'The three circles of the new corporate logo...reflect the company's unique, three-tiered business model as a franchisor, processor and advisor.' Of course. It's staring me in the face. Huawei

Technologies, the Chinese telecoms giant, claimed in a letter to customers that its updated fan-like logo 'reflects Huawei's principles of customer focus, innovation, steady and sustainable growth, and harmony'. Anything else? Not to be outdone, LG, the Korean industrial conglomerate, suggests that 'the letters "L" and "G" in a circle symbolise the World, Future, Youth, Humanity and Technology'.

Such semiotic bombast is unusual. It is even rarer – almost unheard of, in fact – for a business to go the other way and positively prohibit any fancy-dan interpretations of its logo. In 1994, one company – a Swiss insurance company – did. 'The Swiss Re symbol (three thick vertical bars topped by a single horizontal bar) is abstract. It does not represent any image, word or sound. Its four components form a simple, geometrical syntax which is easy to follow and remember.'

A modern logo that doesn't try to mean anything? Now that is unique.

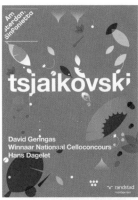

Where do logos go?

<u>Logos have to inhabit a huge range
of environments and branded
applications, and to look at home in
each one.</u>
The designer's skill is
in creating a mark that can adapt
and have impact wherever it might
be applied, from posters, literature,
websites and advertising to banners,
bags, products, packaging, labels,
receipts, uniforms, buildings and,
occasionally, landscapes.

1/ DVD case for media training consultancy Surefire
   (designed by Stylo Design)
2/ Logo as landmark: Illuminated Bayer Cross
   in Leverkusen, Germany
3/ Logo as landscape: KFC's Colonel Sanders
   depicted by 65,000 tiles in the Area 51 desert
   to be visible from space
4/ Moderna Museet in Stockholm, where a signature
   (written by Robert Rauschenberg) becomes
   part of the architecture (identity designed by
   Stockholm Design Lab)
5/ Banner for the Roppongi Hills complex in Tokyo
   (designed by Barnbrook Design)
6/ Toiletries packaging for retailer Åhlens
   (designed by Stockholm Design Lab)
7/ Illuminated sign for alcoholic beverages group
   V&S (design by Stockholm Design Lab)
8/ Posters for Amsterdam Sinfonietta
   (designed by Studio Dumbar)
9/ Banner outside The Whitechapel Gallery, London
   (designed by Spin)

1 2   8
3 4   9
    5
6 7

Contents

Logotypes and letters   Wordmarks and initials

Logotypes and letters   Typographic elements

Symbols   Abstract

Symbols   Representational

Families and sequences

Logotypes and letters

Logos divide themselves into two very broad types. One type is based on text, the other has its roots in pictures.

'Logotypes and letters' brings together logos that use written characters as their starting point. The most obvious examples are logotypes – logos comprising words and names (for example, Kellogg's, Xerox) and acronyms (for instance, RAC, CNN) – and logos that revolve around single letters (for example, United Airlines, Honda). But also included are logos featuring other characters that are used in text: numerals, ampersands, plus signs and such punctuation marks as commas, colons, full stops and accents.

All logos are designed to foster instant recognition, not by what they say but by how they look. Word-based logos are seldom read as text in the way that this text is read. If a logo is visible enough, language ceases to be an issue. That is because the more we see a word or set of letters in a particular typeface, the more it assumes the quality of a visual object rather than text. Alan Fletcher, arguably the godfather of British graphic design, coined the term 'logobility' to describe the potential of a word or words for conversion into a unique typographic device – something for which great logo designers have well-developed antennae.

The distinction between text and symbol blurs further when letters and typographic details are adapted to become representational: a 'b' that is turned into a seat for a furniture company, for example, or an 'h' that doubles as a house in a logo for a homeless charity. As for quotation marks, when are they what they say they are, and when are they speech bubbles?

Wordmarks and initials

Words carry meaning; typefaces convey character. The possible combinations are profuse, and have grown since the advent of electronic font design. Designers working with sophisticated design software have generated thousands of original typefaces and made them available (at a fee) for download, and the best of these can find their way into logos in any part of the world. Classic and 'retro' fonts can be remodelled and tweaked to suit modern applications. Bespoke fonts are frequently commissioned by corporate clients as a means of differentiation. Once the domain of idealistic artists and artisans such as Eric Gill, type design is now one of the most commercialized crafts around.

However, as this section of the book demonstrates, in most cases the choice of typeface is just the start of creating a unique logotype. Words can be cropped, blurred, re-ordered, re-oriented, reversed and rotated. Letters and parts of words can be spaced, emphasized, overlapped, intertwined, illustrated and ornamented. Treatments like these are usually significant; they suggest things about the activities or attributes of the organization being represented, and occasionally about the designers responsible.

For example, logos based on handwriting are popular in industries and professions where the qualities of care and trust are important: food manufacture, healthcare and crafts. Young creative enterprises favour overlapping and joined-up letterforms. Western businesses with a Far Eastern flavour, such as restaurants, tend toward vertically oriented logos. Architects and photographers like three-dimensional word marks. And the fluidity and expressiveness suggested by blurred and treated type works well for arts organizations. The practice of combining and animating letterforms, meanwhile, is almost exclusively the province of designers in the UK and USA.

five

01/

AmericanAirlines®

02/

Kodak

03/

ZMARCHITECTURE

Amrita Jhaveri

01/Five
Terrestrial TV station, UK.
Designed by Spin, 2004
A robust no-nonsense
identity for a populist
channel.

02/American Airlines
Airline, USA. Designed
by Vignelli Associates,
1967
A simple counterpart
to the 'AA' logo with
a stylized eagle.

03/Kodak
Photographic materials
and equipment brand,
USA. Designed by
Brand Integration
Group, 2006
The type-only successor
to the brand's 1971
vintage yellow-and-
red K/arrow symbol
is intended to offer a
'more international and
universal impact', and to
distance the company
from its film and
processing past.

04/ZM Architecture
Architecture practice,
UK. Designed by
Graphical House, 2005
Bespoke type for a
firm that offers one-off
solutions.

05/Amrita Jhaveri
Private gallery
specializing in Indian
art, India. Designed by
Spin, 2006
Redrawn from the
American Typewriter
font, the logo suggests
a fusion of Western and
Eastern cultures.

Fonds 1818

Nykredit

Hoop

06/

07/

08/

A R C H I T E C T U R E
R E S E A R C H
O F F I C E

09/

10/

11/

12/

NUVEEN

belmacz

EimerStahl

13/

14/

15/

B A R N E Y S
N E W Y O R K

Flocafé.

dba

16/

17/

18/

06/Fonds 1818
Charitable foundation,
The Netherlands.
Designed by Studio
Bau Winkel, 2001

07/Nykredit
Financial services,
Denmark. Designed
by Bysted, 1990
One of Denmark's
leading financial
groups, with activities
from mortgages to
estate agency.

08/Hoop
Fashion mall, Japan.
Designed by Taste Inc
(CD: Hitoshi Sasaki,
Atsuo Kishi; AD:
Satoshi Takenaka,
Kozo Sakaemura; D:
Toshiyasu Nanbu), 2000
A name and oval
letterforms that echo the
floorplan of the building.

**09/Architecture
Research Office**
Architecture practice,
USA. Designed by
Open, 2006
Not simply words; read
vertically, the letters
form an acronym of
the company name.

10/OshKosh
Children's clothing,
USA. Designed by
Wolff Olins, 2004
The hard-wearing
clothing company
founded in Oshkosh,
Wisconsin, in 1895 goes
back to its roots with a
sturdy, playful identity.

11/V&S
Alcoholic beverages
group, Sweden.
Designed by Stockholm
Design Lab, 2003
One of the world's
largest ten alcoholic
drinks groups, active
in 125 countries, with
brands including
Absolut.

12/Catalyst
Science and Industry
Council for London,
UK. Designed by
Kent Lyons, 2005

**13/Nuveen Asset
Management**
Municipal bond portfolio
managers, USA.
Designed by Crosby
Associates, 1984

14/Belmacz
Jewelry design,
UK. Designed by
Mind Design, 2000
The collection of Julia
Muggenberg was
named in homage to the
1950s jewelry designer
Suzanne Belperron.
The lettering was
inspired by the sign
on a shop owned by
Muggenberg's mother
in Germany.

15/EimerStahl
Legal practice, USA.
Designed by Crosby
Associates, 2000
Easier and more
balanced than the
full name: Eimer Stahl
Klevorn & Solberg.

16/Barneys New York
Fashion emporium, USA.
Designed by Chermayeff
& Geismar Inc. (D: Steff
Geissbuhler), 1981
Type manages to be
both contemporary and
classic in a logo that is
proud of its NY heritage.

17/Flocafé
Coffee shop chain,
Greece. Designed by
HGV, 2006
The type style creates
the sense of a local café
as opposed to a chain.

18/DBA
Design Business
Association, UK.
Designed by Roundel
(D: John Bateson), 2003
A professional body that
makes links between
design and business,
as reflected in the serif
of the 'd' and 'b'.

19/

NEC

20/

Microsoft®

21/

PHILIPS

THE NATIONAL MUSEUM OF ART, ARCHITECTURE AND DESIGN

—

19/Ether
Digital communications, USA. Designed by Addis Creson, 2006
A typeface that reflects the digital medium in which the company works.

20/NEC
Electronics and IT group, Japan. Designed by Landor Associates, 1992
Known as Nippon Electronic Company up until 1983.

21/Microsoft Corporation
Software group, USA. Designed by Microsoft (D: Scott Baker), 1987
Although the company was originally known (in the 1970s) as Micro-Soft, the slash between the 'o' and 's' conveys the notion of speed.

22/Philips
Electronics and domestic appliances group, The Netherlands. Designed by Louis Christiaan Kalff, 1938
The wordmark is adapted from Philips's original corporate symbol that featured waveforms and stars in a circle.

23/The National Museum of Art, Architecture and Design
Museum, Norway.
Designed by Mission Design, 2004
Norway's national museum was created in 2003 when four former museums united.

k+k
groep

Télérama

24/

25/

26/

bare mobler

27/

LE BONHEUR_
EPICERIE
AUDIO
VISUELLE

Ragne Sigmond

XEROX®

Granite

24/Koppert + Koenis
Architecture and
planning group, The
Netherlands. Designed
by smel, 2006

25/Huey
Electronic colour-control
system from Pantone,
USA. Designed by
G2 Branding & Design
(D: Lou Antonucci), 2004

26/Télérama
Weekly cultural and
listings magazine,
France. Designed by
CDT, 1990
Part of a complete
redesign to attract new,
younger readers.

27/Bare Møbler
Interior and furniture
design, Norway.
Designed by
Grandpeople, 2005
A partnership between
furniture designers Ørjan
Djønne and Karl Marius
Sveen, the company
has a simple and
clean approach with
interesting details.

28/Le Bonheur
Audio-visual 'grocery',
Belgium. Designed by
Coast, 2000
Le Bonheur sells DVDs,
CDs, magazines and art.

29/Per4m
Biannual youth
theatre festival, The
Netherlands. Designed
by The Stone Twins, 2004
A performance festival
organized by Kunst en
Cultuur Noord-Holland.

30/Ragne Sigmond
Photographer and artist,
Denmark. Designed by
Kallegraphics, 2005

31/Xerox
Printing equipment and
software brand, USA.
Designed by Lippincott
Mercer, 1961; letterforms
adjusted by Chermayeff
& Geismar Inc., 1968;
letter spacing and
colour changed by
Landor, 1994.

32/Granite Colour Ltd
Printer, UK. Designed by
Form (AD: Paula Benson,
Paul West; D: Claire
Warner), 2005

M&Co.

GOOD

milk
&one
sugar

34/   35/   36/

37/

33/RAC
Car insurance and recovery services, UK
Designed by North Design, 1997
The introduction of the RAC's radical new logo and identity system in 1994 took millions of British motorists by surprise and revolutionized perceptions of the organization.
By the late 1980s, the RAC (the Royal Automobile Club of Great Britain) was looking like part of a slower bygone era. Its conservative navy-blue livery and traditional crest were no match for the bright yellow vans and bold 'AA' logo of its main rival, the Automobile Association.
To remake its visual identity, it went not to a large branding consultancy but to a new, young, relatively unknown design studio. North created the ultra-modern logotype and high visibility colour palette, and produced designs for every conceivable branded item in a book that has become a collector's item. The transformation in fortunes was instant. Memberships climbed and the profitable RAC Motoring Services was sold to Lex Service. In 2002, Lex, the parent company, changed its name to RAC plc, adopted the identity and applied it to its other companies, BSM and Auto Windscreens.

34/M&Co
Fashion retail chain, UK.
Designed by Arthur-SteenHorneAdamson (D: Marksteen Adamson, Scott McGuffie), 2005
A change of name for 'value' clothes retailer Mackays accompanied a move to more fashionable but still affordable ranges.

35/Good
Business magazine, USA. Designed by Area 17, 2006
Media that pulls no punches about 'the merger of idealism and capitalism'.

36/Milk & One Sugar
Film-production company, USA.
Designed by Malone Design (D: David Malone), 2005
A refreshing absence of Hollywood glitz for this outfit, possibly because most of their time is spent in meetings, drinking tea.

37/3M
Diversified technology, USA. Designed by Siegel & Gale, 1977
Timeless visual simplicity unites the most diverse of businesses. '3M' comes from the group's original name, Minnesota Mining & Manufacturing Company.

01/

02/

03/

04/

MODERNA MUSEET

05/

Carluccio's

Ford

Harrods

06/
07/
08/

olive ®

09/

01/The Walt Disney Company
Media and entertainment group, USA. Designed by Walt Disney, 1940s
An evolved, stylized version of the founder's signature that now identifies a media empire with over $25 billion in annual sales.

03/The Diana, Princess of Wales Memorial Fund
Charitable trust, UK. Designed by Spencer du Bois (D: John Spencer), 1998

02/bzzzpeek.com
Online animal sounds project, UK. Designed by FL@33 (D: Agathe Jacquillat and Tomi Vollauschek), 2002
FL@33 initiated an interactive 'comparison of international onomatopoeia'. Visitors to the site can add their own animal sounds. Bzzzpeek is a submission from France for the sound of a bee.

04/oi polloi
Men's fashion store, UK. Designed by Funnel Creative, 2006
Recently voted best shop in the UK, Manchester-based oi polloi takes its name from the Greek 'hoi polloi', meaning 'the people' or 'the many', and sells democratic, non-fashion clothing.

05/Moderna Museet
National museum of modern art, Sweden. Designed by Stockholm Design Lab with Greger Ulf Nilsson and Henrik Nygren, 2003
Museum as art: original handwriting by Robert Rauschenberg.

06/Carluccio's
Italian restaurant and delicatessen chain, UK. Designed by Kontrapunkt, 1992
Run by Antonio and Priscilla Carluccio, this chain across London and south-east England began with one shop in Covent Garden.

07/Ford
Vehicle-manufacturing group, USA. Designed by CH Wills, 1909; most recently updated by The Partners (AD: Gill Thomas, Nick Clark; D: Nick Eagleton, Nigel Davies), 2003
An engineer and draughtsman, CH Wills worked for Henry Ford in the company's earliest days. The 'centennial' version of the Ford oval, featuring improved legibility, is part of a corporate revitalization strategy.

08/Harrods
Department store, UK. Designed by Minale Tattersfield, 1967 and 1986
In the mid-1960s, there were a dozen different logos in use by the company, each based loosely on a signature. Minale Tattersfield 'took the best one and redesigned it' to create today's well-known identity. The 1986 review made only subtle modifications to address changes in the company and the market.

09/Olive
Digital audio equipment manufacturer, USA. Designed by Liquid Agency

1.2 Handwritten

Johnson & Johnson

 LEICA

10/Kellogg's
Cereals and convenience foods manufacturer, USA
Designed by Will Keith Kellogg, 1906
One of the world's most recognizable wordmarks, the Kellogg's logo is a classic case of using the founder's signature as a guarantee of authenticity in an era when food products were being sold further and further from their place of manufacture. WK Kellogg entered the cereal business just as American eating habits were changing from heavy, fatty breakfasts to lighter, grain-based meals. In 1906, he founded Battle Creek Toasted Corn Flake Company. Each box of flakes bore the words, 'None genuine without this signature' to distinguish its contents from those of the 42 other cereal companies in Battle Creek, Michigan. It also carried the legend, 'The Original'. The company quickly changed its name to Kellogg's, and elevated a highly visible red stylized version of the signature to the top of the pack front, where it has stayed for over 100 years.

11/Stussy
Streetwear label, USA.
Designed by Shawn Stussy, 1980
Shawn Stussy was already shaping and signing surfboards on Laguna Beach, California, when he started to apply his marker pen to T-shirts. From signing clothes, he went into designing them. As the brand has grown, the signature has evolved a little into the current version.

12/Johnson & Johnson
Healthcare products, USA. Designed by James Wood Johnson, 1886
Established in New Jersey (and still with headquarters there) to supply antiseptic surgical dressings, J&J still bears the (modified) signature of one of its founding brothers.

13/Boots
Health and beauty retailer, UK. Designed by Jesse Boot, 1883
Having had a hand in his parents' Nottingham pharmacy since he was 10, Jesse Boot was a born entrepreneur with a flair for marketing, which included making his signature the shop sign.

14/Leica Camera
Camera manufacturer, Germany. Designed by Ernst Leitz II; updated by Stankowski & Duschek, 1995
A mark that commands respect in the world of photography, the red dot logo started life as the signature of Ernst Leitz II, whose factory produced microscope lenses. The company marketed the world's first small-format 35mm camera in the 1920s, calling it the Leica – a contraction of Leitz camera. It was only in the 1980s that the signature in the red dot was changed from Leitz to Leica.

makri

01/

02/   03/   04/

Stereohype™

05/

06/   07/   08/

US
University of Sussex

09/

01/Makri
Jewelry designer,
Greece. Designed
by Spin, 2003
Delicate and linear,
the mark reflects the
contemporary design of
Ileana Makri's creations.

02/Frank
Interior and furniture
design partnership,
UK. Designed by
Multistorey, 2001
For use on furniture,
signs and printed
matter, this logo is the
result of a request for
a mark that would be
visually interesting
whichever way up it
was seen.

03/Nove
Association of Galician
gastronomic chefs,
Spain. Designed by
Area 17, 2004
Inspired by Japanese
seals, the logo was
created for a group of
nine emerging chefs
in Galicia, north-west
Spain. In Spanish, 'nove'
means 'nine' and 'novos'
means 'young'.

04/Ling Ling
Cocktail bar, UK.
Designed by
North Design, 2002
Shades of 1970s
nightclubs are
suggested in this mark
for a sleek, stylish,
Eastern-tinged bar
in the West End of
London, which adjoins
the Hakkasan oriental
restaurant.

05/Stereohype
Online graphic-art and
fashion boutique, UK.
Designed by FL@33 (D:
Agathe Jacquillat and
Tomi Vollauschek), 2004

06/CPP
Personal insurers, UK.
Designed by CDT, 2006
a 'life assistance'
company that provides
protection against card
and mobile-phone theft
and identity fraud, CPP
relaunched in 2006.

07/Land Securities
Property company, UK.
Designed by NB: Studio
(AD: Nick Finney, Ben
Stott, Alan Dye; D: Sarah
Fullerton), 2005
A monogram for a luxury
development formed by
the LS of the company
name.

08/The Flash Express
Rock band, USA.
Designed by Form
(AD: Paul West; D: Nick
Hard), 2004
This three-piece band
on Hit It Now! Records
is influenced by hip hop
and 1960s Stax soul.

09/University of Sussex
Higher-education
establishment, UK.
Designed by Blast, 2004
A unifying identity
replaced over 250
different logos in
use throughout the
institution. It captures
the inclusiveness of the
university's tradition of
internationalism and
social engagement.
In its first year it helped
to deliver an increase
in undergraduate
applications of 23% –
three times the average
of UK universities.

corbis.

M's Wonder

11/

12/

13/

tear

tsunami records

the Modern

14/

15/

16/

10/CN
Railway, Canada
Designed by Allan Fleming, 1960
The most durable and most loved identities are those that do not need to be updated; they seem never to lose their vitality and youth.
The logo for the Canadian National Railway is timeless. The company was seen as old-fashioned and stuck in its ways when it invited Allan Fleming, just 30 at the time, to create its new image. He deliberately avoided literal symbols as he thought they showed their age too soon. 'A literal drawing in 1944 of an object – even a plant leaf – looks in 1954 as if it was drawn in 1944,' he said at the time. To visualize a forward-looking image, he drew on those logos that had best stood the test of time. Inspired by the Christian cross and the Ancient Egyptian symbol for life, Fleming focused on a line of a single thickness. After countless experiments, he hit upon the final fluid letterforms while sketching on a napkin on a flight to New York. The flowing line symbolizes 'the movement of people, materials and messages from one point to another', and was adopted immediately. Within a year, media guru Marshall McLuhan proclaimed the logo 'an icon'.

11/Corbis
Online image licensing, USA. Designed by Segura Inc, 2004
In this design, a leaner lighter look than previously was adopted by the Seattle-based company that started life as Bill Gates's hobby. It is now chasing Getty Images hard for the top spot in the online image library market.

12/M's Wonder
Jewelry design studio, Japan. Designed by Katsuichi Ito Design Studio, 2002

13/Pulp
Health-food restaurant chain, Belgium. Designed by Coast, 1999

14/Tear
Christian anti-poverty relief agency, The Netherlands. Designed by ME Studio, 2006
Tear originally stood for The Evangelical Alliance Relief Identity, now known as the Dutch Tear Fund, but the logo shortens the name to a single word. The ligature between the 'e' and 'a' is intended to represent the unity between north and south, while the crossed 't' carries the Christian message.

15/Tsunami Records
Record shop, Australia. Designed by Sassen Design, 2005
Vinyl dance music is sold online and in the Melbourne store.

16/The Modern
Band, UK. Designed by Form (AD: Paul West; D: Paul West, Claire Warner, Andy Harvey), 2006

01/

ma spruijt

octate

alu°n

02/

03/

04/

05/

envoy

SOULVATION

01/BAD
New-media agency, UK. Designed by Sam Dallyn, 2006

02/Mart Spruijt
Printer, The Netherlands. Designed by Samenwerkende Ontwerpers (D: André Toet, Amie Norman), 2006
For one of The Netherlands' finest printers, established for over a century, a transparent overlay of words conveys the ability to move with the times.

03/Octate
Contemporary furniture manufacturer, USA. Designed by Rob Duncan, 2005
Pure, simple and geometric, the wordmark echoes the style of the company's furniture.

04/Aluin
Theatre group, The Netherlands. Designed by ankerxstrijbos, 2002

05/Melektronikk
Record label, Norway. Designed by Grandpeople, 2004
An experimental music label that is aimed at non-eggheads.

06/Envoy
Dance act, USA/UK. Designed by Graphical House, 2004
Cross-over singer/producer on the Soma Recordings label.

07/Soulvation
Dance band, The Netherlands. Designed by The Stone Twins, 2006

catriona mackechnie

01/

02/

Mozarthaus Vienna

03/

04/

05/

ExxonMobil™

zꝏdango®

01/Catriona MacKechnie
Lingerie store,
USA. Designed by
Bibliotheque, 2005
The client, originally
from Scotland but now
based in New York,
wanted a timeless
and elegant identity.
The custom-made
ligature between the
'c' and the 'k' makes
an idiosyncratic and
feminine wordmark.

02/AED
Agency for the
promotion of
architecture,
engineering and design,
Germany. Designed by
Büro Uebele Visualle
Kommunikation, 2005
A unity of three
disciplines is reflected
in the visual identity.

03/Mozarthaus Vienna
Museum, Austria.
Designed by Pentagram
(D: Justus Oehler), 2006
Formerly known as
the Figarohaus, the
house where Mozart
lived for four years and
composed 'The Marriage
of Figaro', this museum
was renamed on the
250th anniversary of
the composer's death
in 2006. The scripted
'M' weaves in and out
of a Bodoni 'V'; Bodoni
was a contemporary
of Mozart's.

04/Chambers Hotel
New York boutique
hotel, USA. Designed by
Pentagram (D: Michael
Bierut), 2000

05/Tutti
Furniture system from
Haworth, USA. Designed
by North Design, 2002
An identity for a system
based on slatted
aluminium components
that lock together
to create a range of
interior furniture.

06/Exxon Mobil
Energy and
petrochemical group,
USA. Designed by
Lippincott Mercer, 1999
Specifically designed to
draw on the historical
graphic elements of
both Exxon and Mobil
following their merger,
the logo includes
Exxon's interlocking
'X' device and the
upper- and lower-case
typography and the red
'O' of the Mobil identity.
The names were
connected to emphasize
the synergy of 'one
company'.

07/Last Gang
Rock band, UK.
Designed by Malone
Design (D: David
Malone), 2006

08/Under The Influence
Events company.
Designed by Malone
Design (D: David
Malone), 2002

09/Zoodango
Social networking
website, USA. Designed
by Segura Inc, 2006
A site that encourages
professionals to make
contact face-to-face
rather than solely
online.

11/

12/

13/

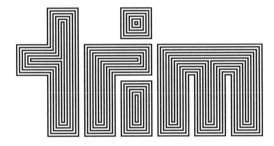

14/

10/conEdison
New York electricity supplier, USA
Designed by Arnell Group, 2000
Utility company logos are ubiquitous in cities, so it is no bad thing when an electricity supplier introduces one that ticks all the boxes of simplicity, originality and memorability.
Consolidated Edison's previous logo had lasted since 1968: the words 'Con' and 'Edison' stacked on top of each other in utilitarian sky-blue Helvetica. Arnell Group, creators of identities for DKNY, Reebok and Banana Republic, developed a logotype that wrapped an 'E' in a 'C', like coiled or insulated cable, and reformatted the name to conEdison, taking the emphasis off the 'Con'. By retaining the Helvetica and the sky blue, the change felt less like a revolution and more like an evolution. Best of all, it immediately felt as if the logo had been around for decades: an instant classic.

11/Coarse Recordings
Independent record label, UK. Designed by Funnel Creative, 2006
Inspired by the copyright symbol, this simple, easy-to-apply, hand-drawn logotype was created for a record label set up by students and staff at City College Manchester.

12/Brett Group
Supplier of aggregates, concrete and landscaping products, UK. Designed by Corporate Edge, 2004

13/Utrecht CS
Promoter of Utrecht, The Netherlands.
Designed by ankerxstrijbos, 2006
A logo for Utrecht's creative network that is part of a visual 'language' consisting of identifiers formed from the letters 'C' and 'S'. These are used on a creative map of the city and other applications.

14/Trim
Film and video editing house, UK. Designed by Multistorey, 2006
Instead of using the obvious images of film and sprockets, Multistorey designed typographic blocks created from concentric linear structures that vibrate visually, almost three-dimensionally, like lines on a monitor.

01/

rabih hage

02/

03/

04/

05/

06/

07/

d-Solutions

08/

09/

10/

11/

01/EMAP Digital Radio
Digital radio stations group, UK. Designed by Roundel (D: John Bateson, Paul Ingle, Keelan Ross), 2004
The negative space of the 'D' forms an appropriately pixellated 'r'.

02/Rabih Hage
Interior designer, UK. Designed by Hat-Trick, 2002
A seamless integration of letterforms that also suggests the handling of light and space.

03/Heinlein Schrock Stearns
Sports architecture practice, USA. Designed by Design Ranch, 2003
'H', 'S' and 'S' on a spinning ball create a sense of movement.

04/National Theatre
National theatre, UK. Designed by FHK Henrion, 1971
An industrialized stencilled identity designed to match the theatre's brutalist home on London's South Bank.

05/VMF Capital
Personal portfolio investment company, USA. Designed by BBK Studio, 1998

06/De Beers LVMH
Diamond jewelry joint venture, UK. Designed by The Partners (AD: Gill Thomas, Aziz Cami, Janet Neil; D: Mike Paisley, Rob Holloway), 2002
The gap between the 'B' and 'D' glints like a gem.

07/Frost & Reed
Fine art dealer, UK. Designed by Atelier Works, 2006
Frost & Reed was established in 1808, and although the art market has evolved since then, the dealer's identity had not. The new identity needed to be 'fresh but conservative'.

08/d-Solutions
Digital solutions company, Japan. Designed by Katsuichi Ito Design Studio, 2004

09/London Symphony Orchestra
Musical company, UK. Designed by The Partners (AD: Nick Clark; D: Martin Lawless), 2001
LSO has led the way in turning classical music from an elitist art form into an accessible contemporary experience. Its logo expresses the music-making flair and fluidity that has been instrumental in the process.

10/Formula One Licensing BV
Formula one motor racing licensor, UK. Designed by Carter Wong Tomlin, 1994
Replacing the different identities of individual race promoters, this mark for the FIA Formula One World Championships ensures consistent branding at each race.

11/USA Network
Cable TV network, USA. Designed by Peloton Design, 2005
The network's fifth identity in 25 years, this is the first not to make reference to stars, stripes, red or blue.

1.6 Combined characters

12/

13/

14/

Copenhagen
Jazz Festival

15/

16/

17/

18/

NEWSPAPER MARKETING AGENCY

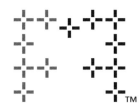

FULTON MARKET FILMS

™

12/Sandhurst Shrubs
Horticultural specialist, UK. Designed by DA Design, 2004

13/UK Japan 2008
Campaign to promote Anglo-Japanese collaboration, UK. Designed by Johnson Banks, 2006
A neat solution for the British Embassy in Tokyo that does the impossible and satisfies both sides without compromise: a bilingual mark that fits the kanji characters for 'nihonkoku' (land of the rising sun) into 'UK'. One of the characters had to be rotated anti-clockwise, but, says Michael Johnson, 'The Japanese are so used to seeing those two kanji characters together, they [can still] read it'.

14/Sherlock Interiors
Interior fit-out contractor, UK. Designed by Brownjohn (D: James Beveridge, Andy Mosley), 2003
An 'S' that conceals an 'i' and demonstrates an eye for detail.

15/Copenhagen Jazz Festival
Music festival, Denmark. Designed by e-types
An identity that is classic or avant-garde, depending on how you look at it – much like the traditional and more contemporary jazz played at the festival.

16/Tischlerei Peters
Bespoke furniture manufacturer, Germany. Designed by Pentagram (D: Justus Oehler)
The 'T' divides the 'P' into three beautifully assembled pieces.

17/Mexico University School of Industrial Design
Higher-education department, Mexico. Designed by Lance Wyman, 1969
Having designed the identity and graphics for the 1968 Mexico Olympics, Lance Wyman created this mark, a model of economy, for the industrial design school of Universidad Nacional Autonoma de México.

18/Radius
Digital solutions, Japan. Designed by Katsuichi Ito Design Studio, 2000

19/Veterans Administration
Government agency devoted to military veterans' affairs, USA. Designed by Malcolm Grear Designers, 1978

20/Models One
Model agency, UK. Designed by The Partners (AD: Nina Jenkins; D: Rob Howsam, Steve Owen, Tony De Ste Croix, Annabel Clements), 1999
The identity for Europe's leading model agency features an 'M' and a 'l' combined...Or is it just a 'l' admiring itself in a mirror?

21/Newspaper Marketing Agency
Marketer of newspapers to advertisers, UK. Designed by SomeOne, 2000
A resemblance to folded sheets and the construction of newspapers is apparent in this combination of letters.

22/Fulton Market Films
Film-production company, USA. Designed by Segura Inc, 2006

1.6 Combined
characters

PLUS®

24/   25/   26/

university college
for the creative arts

27/

23/ FreemanWhite
Architecture, engineering and planning group, USA
Designed by Malcolm Grear Designers, 1999
Characterizing the work of Malcolm Grear
Designers, the logo for FreemanWhite displays
economy and elegance. This small studio in
Providence, Rhode Island, with a reputation that
belies its size, is expert at condensing laborious
acronyms into simple memorable marks that endure
changes in fashion, as its two other projects in this
section also show.
For Malcolm Grear, who established the studio in
1960, this is an art learned only by the study of
typography and individual letterforms. He writes:
'Every letter is not necessarily beautiful when
judged as a single unit. Each letter is companion
to 25 others; some are symmetrical, others
asymmetrical. The beauty of a letter is revealed
by how it meshes with companion parts of a total
typographic system, how it works in combination
with its fellows.'

**24/Hunter Museum of
American Art**
Museum, USA. Designed
by Malcolm Grear
Designers, 2001
The mark was created
as part of the 50th-
anniversary celebrations
of the museum, one of
the leading repositories
of American art.

25/PLUS
Image-licensing
agency, USA. Designed
by Pentagram (CD: Kit
Hinrichs; D: Erik Schmitt),
2005
The Picture Licensing
Universal System (PLUS)
is an international
cooperative multi-
industry initiative that
defines and classifies
image usage.

26/krautheimconcepts
Classical music agency,
Germany. Designed by
Pentagram (D: Justus
Oehler, Uta Tjaden),
2003
A combination of letters
in a roman serif font also
happens to resemble
musical notation.

**27/University College for
the Creative Arts**
Higher-education
institution, UK. Designed
by Blast, 2005
A brand identity for
a new university that
unites Kent Institute of
Art & Design and the
Surrey Institute of Art
& Design University
College. The system
allows individual
campuses and students
to customize the mark
by making their own
work the cutaway for
the combined 'c' and 'a'.

CENTRE

01/

02/

COLOURSET

03/

marianne mi1ani
couture

Paddington
Walk

01/CT Centre
Counter-Terrorism
Science & Technology
Centre, UK. Designed
by Roundel (D: Adam
Browne, Mike Denny,
Simon John), 2006
A dedicated unit formed
to offer scientific and
technical advice to
UK and international
authorities, with a
logotype that reflects its
positioning statement:
'seeing the unseen'.

**02/Chesterton
International**
Estate agent, UK.
Designed by The
Partners (AD: Nina
Jenkins, Tim Prior;
D: Bob Young, Sophie
Hayes), 2005
For a company that
wants to express its
knowledge of the market
and of housing history,
this mark makes the
agency's own heritage
– established in London,
1805 – manifest.

03/Colourset Litho
Printer, UK. Designed by
Kino Design, 2003
A logo that when
turned on its side
provides a platform for
the printer to become
more personal and
possessive about his
standards and service.

04/Milani 1a Couture
Couturier, Switzerland.
Designed by Atelier
Bundi, 1988

05/Paddington Walk
Residential
development, UK.
Designed by ico
Design, 2003
A development of
London city apartments,
or 'pads', by European
Land.

Dim²⁄₃₄nsions

AQUALISA

CATERPILLAR®

01/

02/

03/

PIRELLI

04/

ripple**ffect**
SOUND DESIGN

FIRST BOOKING

05/

06/

07/

MS
Multiple Sclerosis Society

see

QUINTET

Mobil®

01/Dimensions
Exhibitions and signage company, UK. Designed by Johnson Banks, 1994 The numbers connect with the company's systems (D2, D3 and D4) and with its multidimensional displays.

02/Aqualisa
Shower manufacturer, UK. Designed by Carter Wong Tomlin, 2004 Aqualisa wanted an identity that conveyed what it was about, something its previous logo failed to do. Fortunately, its thermostatic control made a perfect 'Q'.

03/Caterpillar Inc
Manufacturer of construction and mining equipment, USA. Designer unknown Famous first for making the 'caterpillar' tracks that served Allied tanks in World War I, the company is better known today for machines that move earth, rocks and minerals – in the manner of the 'A' in its logotype. It was this heavy-duty brand image that enabled the company to diversify into hard-wearing boots, clothing and accessories.

04/Pirelli
Industrial group, Italy. Designed by Pirelli, 1908 A distinctive stretched 'P' for the Milan-based company that started out in life as a tyre and cable maker and has now moved into property, photonics and new materials.

05/Rippleffect Sound Design
Sound engineers, Canada. Designed by Hambly & Woolley Inc (CD: Bob Hambly; DD: Barb Woolley; D: Philip Mondor), 2005

06/HNTB Corporation
Architecture, engineering and construction group, USA. Designed by Siegel & Gale, 2003 The two components of the 'H' create a perfect fit.

07/First Booking
Talent agency for make-up artists and stylists, Denmark. Designed by Designbolaget, 2004 Nothing to do with football, the agency provides top talent to the advertising and film-production industries.

08/Multiple Sclerosis Society
Charity, UK. Designed by Spencer du Bois (John Spencer), 1999

09/See
Personal investment brand, UK. Designed by Brownjohn (D: James Beveridge), 2006 Transparent and accessible, says SEI Investments of their package for pensions and savings.

10/Quintet
Advertising agency, The Balkans. Designed by HGV, 2004 An agency with five partners, in case you missed the emphasis on five.

11/Mobil
Fuels and lubricating oils brand, USA. Designed by Chermayeff & Geismar Inc., 1964 Made memorable by its 'o', which, in colour, is red and, in black and white, is two concentric circles that suggest motion and mobility, this is the simplest of logotypes. Since the merger of Exxon and Mobil in 1999, Mobil continues as a brand name within the combined company.

Shelter

FOO🍲ING™   THE OVƎN   GOLDSMITHS
SINCE 1778

13/   14/   15/

Olympiastadion Berlin

16/

12/Shelter
Housing and homeless charity, UK
Designed by Johnson Banks, 2003
Formed in 1966, Shelter comprised five church housing trusts that united to tackle the UK's growing homeless crisis. Initially it was known as Shelter, The National Campaign for Homeless People. Families, such as the one depicted in the film 'Cathy Come Home' (which acted as an alarm call to its British TV audience), were being forced into a life on the streets by an inadequate benefits system, rapacious landlords and slum conditions. Shelter set about righting these wrongs, and improving the standard of housing and temporary accommodation. Approaching its 40th anniversary, however, the charity was still mainly associated with homelessness, and it wanted to correct the balance to reflect its mission to help the 900,000 people still living in substandard housing. Johnson Banks simply put a pitched roof on the 'H' to tell the story in an instant.

13/Fooing
Food-oriented teambuilding company, UK. Designed by Elmwood, 2003
The experience of food preparation, tasting and appreciation is turned into a motivational tool.

14/The Oven
Sales promotion agency UK. Designed by Unreal, 2004

15/Goldsmiths
Jewelry retail chain, UK. Designed by The Partners (AD: Nina Jenkins, Tim Prior, Nick Eagleton; D: Helen Cooley, Sue Farringdon, Claire Turner), 2003
With a 225-year history and over 170 stores selling high quality watches and fine jewelry, Goldsmiths was surprised to find that many shoppers had never heard of it. Its new identity and retail overhaul were conceived to turn around the situation.

16/Olympiastadion Berlin
Olympic stadium, Germany. Designed by Büro für Gestaltung Wangler & Abele, 2000
When Berlin's Olympic Stadium was refurbished for the 2006 World Cup, a roof was added with an opening at the end of the marathon gate; a distinguishing feature gently alluded to in the building's logotype.

1.9 Incomplete
characters

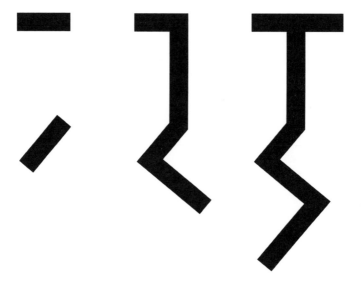

OXIGENO

BASIS

⌐ DT Design Tech

EUROPA

covepark

01/Treasury Shigemura
Architecture practice, Japan
Designed by Taste Inc, 1995
Kanji characters appear so alien to Western eyes that Japanese companies with an interest in international markets are advised to employ other non-written means to articulate their identity. Graphic designers in Japan have had to master the art of designing logos that work on purely visual terms, often through abstract forms and striking colours. Toshiyasu Nanbu, who established his office, Taste Inc, in Osaka in 1988, approaches graphic design as the expression of an 'international language'. No brand that he has designed better demonstrates this than the one that brought him to international attention in 1995. Devised for an architect's office, it seems at first glance like a series of Japanese characters or meaningless minimalist squiggles. When the penny drops –the final element is the letters 'T' and 'S' joined as one – the sequence looks more like stages in an animation or construction, and makes perfect poetic sense.

02/Oxigeno
Fitness centre, Norway.
Designed by Mission Design, 2005

03/Basis
Market research company, UK. Designed by Johnson Banks, 1995
For a firm whose research provides the basis for their clients' projects, the logotype offers enough information to allow the viewer to fill in the rest.

04/Design Tech Jürgen R Schmid
Industrial designer, Germany. Designed by Stankowski & Duschek, 1986
A designer who takes projects from the first stages to the finished article.

05/CEPT (Conference of European Postal and Telecommunications Administration)
Umbrella organization for Europe's regulatory authorities, The Netherlands. Designed by Atelier Bundi, 1991

06/Darkside FX
Film effects company, UK. Designed by Form (AD: Paul West; D: Paul West, Chris Hilton), 2001

07/Cove Park
Arts residency centre, UK. Designed by Graphical House with Sarah Tripp, 2004
Bespoke open lettering conveys the unrestricted and open nature of the residencies and events at this centre, set in the wilds of western Scotland.

1.10 Cropped

sciencecité
wissenschaft
und gesellschaft
im dialog

science et société
en dialogue

scienze e società
in dialogo

ARC

**URBAN
STRATEGIES
INC** ■

01/

02/

03/

Gate.

NoblesGate. Nobles

Film & Television Production

04/

Am
sterdam
Sinfonietta

cutcost.com

05/

06/

07/

Blink CROP VISION

5HN

01/Science et Cité
Foundation to
encourage debate
between society and
the world of science,
Switzerland. Designed
by Atelier Bundi, 2004

02/ARC Representation
Photographers'
representative, USA.
Designed by Marc
English Design, 2004

**03/Urban
Strategies Inc.**
Planning and urban
design firm, Canada.
Designed by Hambly
& Woolley (CD: Bob
Hambly; DD: Barb
Woolley; D: Emese
Ungar-Walker), 2005
Why stick to the grid
when you're a firm with
a reputation for being
creative with city street
plans and structures?

04/Nobles Gate
TV production company,
UK. Designed by
Graphical House, 2004
Intended to function
primarily as an on-
screen identity, the logo
also gives a sense
of animation and
dynamism when seen
in print.

**05/Amsterdam
Sinfonietta**
Independent music
ensemble, The
Netherlands. Designed
by Studio Dumbar, 2006
A logo (and poster
series) designed to draw
a younger audience
to a group previously
seen as traditional,
introverted and distant.

06/cutcost.com
Business procurement
website, UK. Designed
by Thomas Manss &
Company, 2001
Saving its clients money,
this company channels
all orders through
a single 'intelligent'
sourcing system,
thereby securing larger
wholesale orders and
lower prices.

07/Denk Art
Personal development
and counselling agency,
Switzerland. Designed
by Atelier Bundi, 1998
Different personalities,
different behaviours,
different characters:
this agency does not
fit comfortably within
prescribed parameters.

08/Blink
Tile design studio,
UK. Designed by
Kino Design, 2005
Blink and you might
miss the subtle imprints
of everyday items and
icons on this studio's
handmade tiles.

09/Crop
A series of image
catalogues from Corbis,
USA. Designed by
Segura Inc, 2004
An award-winning series
of catalogues featuring
striking photography
from the Corbis
image library, Crop
is intended to banish
the company's dismal
perception among
designers. The name
can be understood as a
reference to the harvest
of imagery in each issue
or as a challenge to
creatives to improve the
images' composition.

10/Vision
Journal of morals and
ethics, USA. Designed
by CDT, 2005
A quarterly journal,
published online and
in print, that explores
new horizons in the
debate about current
social issues.

11/SHN
Theatrical entertainment
company, USA.
Designed by Addis
Creson, 2005
Raising the curtain
on new plays and
Broadway productions.

hygena

01/

02/

03/

04/

Bedrock

05/

06/

07/

Building**Brands**

FUSE

01/Hygena
Kitchen furniture and fittings company, France. Designed by Bibliotheque, 2006
Reflecting the flexibility demanded of built-in kitchen furniture, an 'h' upturned makes a 'y'.

02/Geelong Gallery
Art gallery, Australia. Designed by GollingsPidgeon
Words turn and meander as if wandering through the gallery's exhibition spaces.

03/me studio
Graphic-design agency, The Netherlands. Designed by me studio, 2005
A studio of two – Martin (Pyper) and Erik (Olde Hanhof) – that likes to turn things upside down and back to front.

04/You Turn Training
Training and motivation courses organizer, UK. Designed by Arthur-SteenHorneAdamson (D: Marksteen Adamson, Scott McGufhe), 2003
A training company that helps to take the stress out of such everyday challenges as looking after the car, the house and the kids.

05/Bedrock Records
Record label, UK. Designed by Malone Design (D: David Malone), 1998
An inversion of the glyph '8', used in written German.

06/Banana Republic
Casual clothing chain, USA. Designed by Arnell Group

07/Food Food
Food-oriented radio station, UK. Designed by Unreal, 2006
Dinner for four?

08/Film London East
Support agency for film and media enterprises, UK. Designed by Arthur-SteenHorneAdamson (D: Marksteen Adamson, Scott McGufhe), 2005
A simple visual twist to point audiences in the right direction.

09/Building Brands
Branding consultancy, Germany. Designed by Pentagram (D: Justus Oehler, Uta Tjaden), 2003

10/Shake interactive
Digital marketing agency, UK. Designed by Unreal, 2006

11/Feed
Online journal of opinion, USA. Designed by Chermayeff & Geismar Inc. (D: Jonathan Alger), 2000

12/Dell Inc
Personal computer manufacturer, USA. Designed by Siegel & Gale, 1992
By marketing computer systems directly to consumers in the late 1980s, the maverick Michael Dell stood the PC industry on its ear. In 1992, his company got a logo that said as much in one letter.

13/Fuse
Industrial design firm, USA. Designed by Sandstrom Design, 2000

1.11 Reversals and
rotations

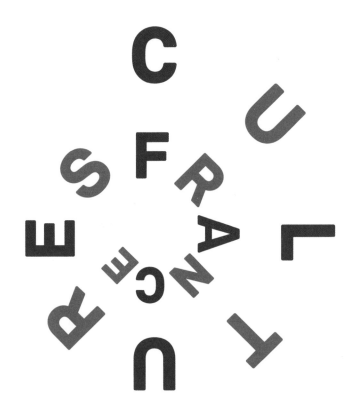

SAL
MANN

15/   16/   17/

ha✕kasan

18/

14/Cultures France
Government agency promoting French culture abroad, France
Designed by Studio Apeloig, 2006
'In order to succeed, graphic design demands the clear thinking of a designer who can combine words and pictures to achieve something distinctive, or useful, or playful, or surprising, or subversive. The designer's goal is to produce something memorable.' Philippe Apeloig is one designer who values visual ideas above computer-generated decoration. Having made his name designing for Paris's Musée D'Orsay in the 1980s, Apeloig honed his typographic sensibilities in California, under the digital graphics pioneer April Greiman. Recently, Apeloig's posters and logos, mostly for cultural institutions and events, have turned toward a stripped-down, almost primitive simplicity. 'My design philosophy is to communicate directly with a poetic attitude.' His logo for the French government's new agency to promote 'international cultural exchanges' is in this vein, taking the form of a Catherine wheel firework when animated, spinning and (it is hoped) sparking new cultural activity in all directions.

15/FL@33
Graphic-design studio, UK. Designed by FL@33 (D: Agathe Jacquillat, Tomi Vollauschek), 2004
A partnership formed by a pair of like-minded graphic designers (one French, one Austrian) at the Royal College of Art.

16/Born and Bread
Organic bakery, UK. Designed by Multistorey, 2003
The kind of decorative monotype that is reminiscent of Biba and other early 1970s retailers. A pair of Bs makes a nice slice of a handmade loaf.

17/Autohaus Salzmann
Volkswagen dealership, Germany. Designed by Stankowski & Duschek, 1987

18/Hakkasan
Oriental restaurant, UK. Designed by North Design, 2001
The character created when the two 'k's share an ascender resembles the Chinese symbol for prosperity; a useful attribute when dining at this sophisticated London eaterie.

1.12 Symmetry and
ambigrams

01/

02/ 03/ 04/

05/

01/Voca
Financial transaction processor, UK. Designed by North Design, 2004
A former agency of the British government, Voca provides payment services to banks and businesses. For applications on credit cards, its logo can be read either way up.

02/Tim Wood Furniture
Furniture designer and maker, UK. Designed by Thomas Manss & Company, 1993
Applied to the furniture itself as well as to the company literature, this modern maker's mark is for a designer who works on bespoke pieces to exacting standards of craftsmanship.

03/Voice of America
Multilingual international broadcasting service, USA. Designed by Chermayeff & Geismar Inc. (D: Steff Geissbuhler), 2004
Making itself heard around the world, Voice of America has a weekly audience of 115 million.

04/Oasen
Drinking-water supplier, The Netherlands. Designed by Total Identity (SD: Aad van Dommelen, Léon Stolk), 2006
Another ambigram, reading identically upside down, but this time a proper name rather than an acronym. The droplet-like opening in the 'o' makes the 'n' possible.

05/RCA
Consumer electronics brand, USA. Designed by Lippincott Mercer, 1960s
When this logo, with its confident distinctive letterforms, was designed, RCA (formerly the Radio Corporation of America) was a business at the peak of its powers, making televisions, recording equipment and other electronics, as well as running a major record label. The troubled company was sold and broken up in the 1980s, but a much smaller RCA consumer electronics business still carries the LM-designed brand.

06/Aspire
Premium travel agency, UK. Designed by Bibliotheque
A crafted ligature between the 'a' and 's' of 'aspire' creates a useful stand-alone stamp of quality for this high-end travel company.

07/VIA Trader
Financial data analyser, UK. Designed by 300million (CD: Nigel Davies; D: Natalie Bennet, Clare Holmes), 2005
Markets can go down as well as up...

08/303
Arts review, France. Designed by Studio Apeloig, 2006
A dynamic and contemporary logo and layout for a highbrow journal.

09/VIV
Agricultural trade fair, The Netherlands. Designed by ankerxstrijbos, 1996
A mark for the Royal Dutch Jaarbeurs exhibition and conference centre.

1.13 Stacked

GE
GEN
W
ART

01/

mi
zu
to.
ri

original japanese geta

02/

spacedout

03/

04/

05/

VIESSMANN

06/

châ
THÉÂTRE
-te-
MUSICAL
let
DE PARIS

07/

TOWN
MVP

C
O
U
Q
O

08/ ....

09/ ....

10/ ....

EN

O

11/ ....

01/Museum Gegenwart
Contemporary art museum, Switzerland. Designed by Atelier Bundi, 2005

02/Mizutori
Japanese geta sandal manufacturer, Japan. Designed by Mind Design, 2005
Specifically designed to help market this company's traditional and modern geta sandals (the kind worn by geisha) in Europe, the logo breaks the name into syllables that, in Japanese, would each be represented by a kanji character.

03/Spaced Out
Architects and product designers, UK. Designed by Mind Design, 2000

04/Busaba Eathai
Thai restaurants, UK. Designed by North Design, 2000
Ethnic futurism: a logo with an appropriately noodle-like quality, running vertically in the manner of Thai calligraphy.

05/Viessmann
Heating systems, Germany. Designed by Stankowski & Duschek, 1960
A word mark with warmth designed by Anton Stankowski, one of the fathers of modernist graphic design. Despite the relatively specialized nature of Viessmann's business, its logo is familiar in Germany and beyond.

06/Châtelet
Theatre and opera house, France. Designed by Studio Apeloig, 2005

07/Town MVP
Social networking website, USA. Designed by Rob Duncan
Sports fans are able to find, manage and play games in their own neighbourhoods by using this website.

08/Drammen
City of Drammen, Norway. Designed by Grandpeople, 2005
Created for an experiment to test whether young people in Drammen would wear the name of their city, which has suffered from a poor reputation in Norway.

09/Levi Strauss & Co.
Apparel company, USA. Designed by Levi Strauss & Co, 1936
An unusual, if not unique, identity by virtue of its 2D representation of a 3D product detail. As the ® symbol sits on the fold of the red tab ribbon it is only partly seen in the 2D graphic. The tab was first seen in 1936, when the company attached it to the right rear pocket of its Levi's® 501® jeans to differentiate them at a distance from the dark denim jeans of its rivals.

10/Couqo
Café, Japan. Designed by Marvin, 2005
Intended to capture a flavour of both traditional and modern Kyoto.

11/English National Opera
Opera house and company, UK. Designed by CDT, 1992
An identity that sings in every sense, and which played a major part in the increase in ENO's audiences and sponsorships.

01/

02/

03/

04/

05/

06/

07/

08/

09/

BABYGRAND HOTELS

™

01/Usual Suspects
Brand entertainment and events organizers, The Netherlands. Designed by The Stone Twins, 2003
Primarily working for the advertising industry, Amsterdam-based Usual Suspects organize events and parties.

02/Data Roger
Freelance web developer, Norway. Designed by Kallegraphics, 2005

03/Federal Signal
Equipment and machinery provider for public services, USA. Designer unknown

04/ABF
French society of librarians, France. Designed by Studio Apeloig, 2006
A well-spaced mark for the Association des Bibliothécaires Français.

05/Eight
Corporate communications agency, UK. Designed by Stylo Design (AD, D: Tom Lancaster), 2005
Eight employees make up this London start-up, whose logo comprises pieces of eight.

06/Intersection
Seminar series, UK. Designed by Blast, 2006
Created for Artquest, an advice and information service for artists and craftspeople, Intersection focuses on the collaboration between artists, designers and companies. Hence a logo in which the whole is greater than the sum of its parts.

07/IMA Shopping Center
Retail complex, Japan. Designed by Katsuichi Ito Design Studio, 1987

08/GAU
Meeting place/workshop for visual artists, The Netherlands. Designed by smel, 2002
'Grafisch Atelier Utrecht' provides facilities and space for local artists and designers.

09/Palm Beach Pediatric Dentistry
Dental practice, USA. Designed by Crosby Associates, 2005
A cheerful mark to make a child's visit to the dentist as much fun as it possibly can be.

10/BabyGrand Hotels
Hotel group, UK. Designed by SomeOne (D: Simon Manchipp, David Law), 2006

11/Astoria
Cinema chain, Sweden. Designed by Stockholm Design Lab, 2005

12/Matador
Architecture studio, Belgium. Designed by Coast, 2004
To emphasize the studio's uncompromisingly modernist approach, Coast designed a font based on Wim Crouwel's modular alphabets.

13/DMAX
Terrestrial TV channel, Germany. Designed by Spin, 2006
A channel aimed specifically at men with a no-messing logo to reflect the testosterone-fuelled programming.

1.14 Modular

14/

15/

16/

17/

18/

19/

20/

21/

22/

14/Richard File
DJ and recording artist,
UK. Designed by Malone
Design (D: David
Malone), 2006

15/BEEM
Contemporary
bridalwear, UK.
Designed by 300million
(D: Martin Lawless), 2004
One shape, three
different letters. Beem
offers bridal couture
for women wanting a
chic, sophisticated and
strictly non-traditional
wedding.

16/GlassLab
Contemporary glass
furniture design studio,
UK. Designed by Funnel
Creative, 2004

17/MexiPi
Management
consultancy, The
Netherlands. Designed
by NLXL, 2006

18/Hive
Hair salon, UK. Designed
by Mind Design, 2006
Lettering 'inspired by
honeycombs' forms
a logo that is applied
in many different
variations.

19/Wodonga
City of Wodonga,
Australia. Designed by
GollingsPidgeon
For Wodonga Council
in provincial Victoria, a
custom-made geometric
typeface was created
on the theme of links
(business-to-business,
council-to-community).
From it, a system of
symbols and icons was
developed to denote
civic and business
functions in the city.

20/DAAM
Architecture and design
practice, UK. Designed
by NB: Studio (AD: Nick
Finney, Ben Stott, Alan
Dye; D: Jodie Wightman),
2003
A mark based on Fregio
Mecano, a modular
typeface designed in
Italy in the 1920s that
allows each character
to be individually
configured at different
proportions.

21/Kepco
Electricity supplier,
South Korea. Designer
unknown

22/Blood
Contemporary art
membership club, UK.
Designed by Value And
Service, 2004
Under the aegis of
the Contemporary Art
Society, Blood organizes
events, talks and tours
for new art lovers and
collectors.

1.14 Modular

Sumi Management

23/

24/

25/

26/

the meeting place . truro

Change tomorrow today

27/

28/

29/

23/Abby CPH
Beauty clinic, Denmark.
Designed by
Designbolaget, 2005

24/Sumi Management
Music artist
management company,
Germany. Designed
by Malone Design
(D: David Malone,
Nick Tweedie), 2004
Using the same single
form in different
configurations, the logo
builds the four letters of
the name into an almost
abstract collage.

25/R.gen
Property developer, UK.
Designed by Funnel
Creative, 2003

26/Turn
Internet advertising
network, USA. Designed
by Addis Creson, 2005
Turn is an online
advertising service
that gathers data
about users' interactions
with advertisers'
websites, and can
therefore better target
its clients' ads. Turns
clicks into customers,
in other words.

27/Indaba
Café bar, UK. Designed
by Absolute Design, 2003

**28/Parsons Brinckerhoff
Inc**
Engineering and
infrastructure services,
USA. Designed by
OH& Co, 2006

29/Plywood
Rock band, Norway.
Designed by
Kallegraphics, 2004

**30/Avaya
Communication**
Business telecoms
technology service,
USA. Designed by
Templin Brink Design
(CD: Joel Templin,
Gaby Brink; D: Felix
Sockwell), 1999

31/Oracle Mobile
Oracle's mobile
technology division,
USA. Designed by
Templin Brink Design
(CD: Joel Templin,
Gaby Brink; D: Brian
Gunderson), 2005

32/Dansk Byggeri
National construction
industry association,
Denmark. Designed by
Bysted, 2003

33/NUD
Electronica band,
Norway. Designed by
Kallegraphics, 2003

34/Sun Microsystems
Computers, software
and IT services, USA.
Designed by Vaughan
Pratt, 1982
Pratt was a Professor
Emeritus in computer
science at Stanford
University when, in 1982,
graduate student Andy
Bechtolsheim built his
68000 Unix System for
the Stanford University
Network. The project
initials became the
name of the company
that Bechtolsheim set
up with fellow students,
and Pratt designed
a logo featuring four
interleaved copies
of the word 'sun' by
breaking the 'S' into
two components.

35/Root
Neighbourhood wellness
centre, USA. Designed
by Sandstrom Design,
2005

1.14 Modular

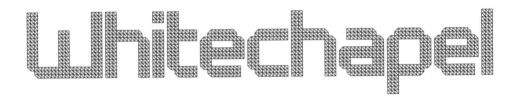

37/ 38/ 39/

40/

36/Whitechapel Gallery
Contemporary art gallery, UK
Designed by Spin, 2003
Approaching a £10-million refurbishment
programme, the Whitechapel Gallery took the
decision not to refresh but to completely re-
conceive its visual identity. Previous identities had
paid too much reverence to the Arts and Crafts
building that houses the gallery, and had failed
to reflect the Whitechapel's influential position
in the field of contemporary art. The new mark
needed to speak up visually for the Whitechapel
in its frenetic inner-city east London setting, while
still allowing the character and content of the
displays to be conveyed on posters, literature
and catalogues. It was a breakthrough project
for the young emerging design studio Spin, who
developed a new character set for the logo and
display texts based on tiny triangular and square
building blocks whose collective transparency can
be turned up or down by varying the weight and
colour of the line. The logo can take centre stage,
or it can take more of a back seat to a full-bleed
art image on an exhibition poster, for example.
But, like the best, most challenging art, it will never
sit quietly in a corner.

37/VIIV
Home entertainment
software service, USA.
Designed by Addis
Creson, 2006
Viiv is Intel's premier
brand for enabling
room-to-room
digital entertainment
through PCs.

38/Lean Alliance
International business
network, Germany.
Designed by Thomas
Manss & Company, 2005
A group of companies
united by their pursuit
of lean management
principles and by a
lean logo based on an
abstract 1960s typeface.

39/Viva
Production studio,
Norway. Designed by
Kallegraphics

**40/Women In Music
Creative Women**
Music recording label,
UK. Designed by
Funnel Creative, 2006

01/

02/

03/

04/

05/

06/

07/

08/

09/

mimUᴚA   HDLG

01/Sky HD
High-definition TV channel, South Korea. Designed by Fitch

02/Søren Rønholt
Photographer, Denmark. Designed by Designbolaget, 2004

03/Paul Maas
Interior architects, The Netherlands. Designed by NLXL, 2006

04/Lund + Slaatto
Architecture practice, Norway. Designed by Mission Design, 2006

05/MTV
Cable TV network, USA. Designed by Manhattan Design (D: Frank Olinsky, Pat Gorman, Patty Rogoff), 1981
An asymmetrical, spray-painted logo: about as far removed as it was possible to be in 1981 from the CBS eye and NBC peacock.

06/Match
Safety-match manufacturer, Japan. Designed by Kokokumaru (D: Yoshimaru Takahashi), 2003

07/Energetica
National centre for energy, The Netherlands. Designed by Samenwerkende Ontwerpers (D: André Toet, Rich Sellars), 2006

08/The Broadway Line
Information phone line, USA. Designed by Open, 1997
Information about productions in New York and on tour across the USA is offered on this toll-free hotline.

09/Mecklenburgh Opera
Musical theatre, UK. Designed by Johnson Banks, 1998
A stage set for two artforms: opera ('O') and music theatre ('M').

10/Tomoharu Mimura
Photographer, Japan. Designed by Taste Inc, 2000

11/HDLC
Architectural lighting company, USA. Designed by Open, 2004

12/Free Library of Philadelphia
Educational institutions and libraries, USA. Designed by Siegel & Gale, 2005
A city-wide network of facilities newly enhanced by this identity and a headquarters – the historic Central Library – remodelled by architect Moshe Safdie.

13/Quart 05
Annual music festival, Norway. Designed by Mission Design, 2005

14/

15/

16/

®

17/

18/

19/

20/

14/Marius Martinussen
Visual artist, Norway.
Designed by
Kallegraphics, 2005

15/GoGo Images
Royalty-free stock
photography service,
USA. Designed by
Segura Inc, 2006
Multicultural imagery
is the focus of this
picture library.

**16/Commission for
Architecture and the
Built Environment**
Government agency for
architecture, planning
and open space, UK.
Designed by Johnson
Banks, 2005
A succinct visual
metaphor for CABE's
three fields of activity
proved elusive, so
its new identity hints
at 3D structures and
arrangements.

**17/Osaka Port
Corporation**
Port authority,
Japan. Designed
by Kokokumaru
(D: Yoshimaru
Takahashi), 2000

18/Sony PlayStation
Video game console
brand, Japan. Designed
by Sony (D: Manabu
Sakamoto), 1994

**19/Commune di Torre
Pellice**
Tourism promotion,
Italy. Designed by
Brunazzi Associati (D:
Giovanni Brunazzi), 2002
An identity for the town
of Torre Pellice, near
Turin, in northern Italy.

**20/Rytmisk
Arrangørpool**
Music producers,
Norway. Designed by
Grandpeople, 2006
Created for producers
at the Rikskonsertene,
which arranges public
concerts in Norway
and abroad.

1.16 Treated

pro audito   THE NEW SCHOOL   AURORA

02/   03/   04/

05/

01/Tate
Art galleries, UK
Designed by Wolff Olins, 1999
In 1998, the Tate Gallery had a problem. There
wasn't just one Tate any more, but three (at
Millbank in London, Liverpool and St Ives) and
each one had its own focus. Plus, there was the
small matter of a fourth gallery on the way in
2000 at the converted Bankside power station.
So, in June the Tate hired Wolff Olins to develop
a Tate brand, one that was less oriented around
the institution and its collection of pictures and
more suggestive of an accessible forward-looking
experience in which all ways of looking at art
would be welcomed. Wolff Olins recommended
dropping the definite article from the name and
giving each location its own identity within the
family: Tate Britain, Tate Liverpool, Tate St Ives
and Tate Modern. A range of logos was created
by modelling the word 'TATE' to shift in and out of
focus, reflecting a dynamic point of view. In the
year following the brand's introduction and Tate
Modern's opening, visitor figures to Tate galleries
rose from 3 million to 7.5 million.

02/Pro Audito
Association for the
hard of hearing,
Switzerland. Designed
by Atelier Bundi, 1995

03/The New School
University, USA.
Designed by Siegel &
Gale, 2005
This urban university
in Greenwich Village
has 'its own distinctive
voice...as direct as
billboards and graffiti'.
Each of its eight schools
has been renamed to
incorporate the umbrella
name (for example,
Parsons The New School
for Design) and given its
own gritty identity.

04/Aurora Orchestra
Chamber orchestra,
UK. Designed by The
Partners (AD: Nick
Eagleton, Nick Clark;
D: Kerry Ostermeyer,
Claire Turner), 2005
With a name inspired by
the colour and energy of
the Aurora Borealis, this
ensemble is composed
of some of the world's
best young players.

05/Syn
Recording studio,
Japan. Designed by
North Design, 2004
Built in Tokyo by Simon
and Yasmin Le Bon and
Nick Wood (S, Y and N),
the studio has interiors
by Marc Newson.

01/

02/

03/

04/

05/

06/

07/

  **SARDEGNA**

01/Troublemaker Studios
Film studio, USA. Designed by Marc English Design, 2001
Film studio owned by Robert Rodriguez.

02/Austin Studios
Film-production company, USA. Designed by Marc English Design, 2000

03/DKNY
Fashion brand, USA. Designed by Arnell Group, 1989
Moving the Statue of Liberty uptown was a good move when it came to attracting metropolitan women to Donna Karan's second brand.

04/Hazlitz
Bespoke stationer, UK. Designed by Browns, 2006
Based on paper stacks, the typeface allows the company to show off its expertise on its own stationery, which is produced using a range of such techniques as litho, debossing and foiling.

05/Wee Gems
Scriptwriting talent scheme, UK. Designed by Graphical House, 2006
Created for BBC Scotland's search for talented new TV writers of children's drama.

06/Tara
Band, Norway. Designed by Kallegraphics, 2006

07/DKV
Private health insurer, Germany. Designed by Metadesign, 2003
Subliminal imagery, or suggestions of imagery, can have a powerful effect. This logo emerged with top marks from an extensive evaluation process and acceptance studies in which the clarity, appeal and salience of different designs (including those of the competition) were assessed.

08/Vanilla Patisserie
Patisserie, UK. Designed by HGV, 2005

09/Natural History Museum
Museum of the natural world, UK. Designed by Hat-Trick Design, 2004
Dramatic changes at the museum necessitated a new identity to reflect a more forward-looking accessible programme. The 'N' provides a window on nature, using stunning images of the earth.

10/Sardegna
Autonomous region, Italy. Designed by Pentagram (D: Justus Oehler), 2006
No sun, sea or sand in sight. A wordmark that combines the modernity of the typeface (based on Eurostile Heavy by Aldo Novarese) with such traditional elements as the patchwork of colours used to embroider Sardinian costumes.

11/Trongate 103
Arts centre, UK. Designed by Graphical House and Sarah Tripp, 2006
Commissioned by Glasgow City Council and Trongate 103 Partners, this identity for a centre housing galleries and artists' spaces features a custom-designed icon set (see 'GATE').

abacus

WAYOUT

02/

03/

04/

VENISE

FILM LON S DON

SIDETRACK™ FILMS

05/

06/

07/

01/CNN
Cable TV news network, USA
Designer unknown
No other advertiser's brand – or TV channel, for that matter – has made such an indelible mark on the minds of viewers as the CNN logo. It was probably created – or commissioned – by Reese Schonfeld, the journalist who co-founded Cable News Network with businessman Ted Turner in 1980 and built its 24-hour broadcasting capability. The channel needed a logotype that suggested seamless continuity, connections, polish and power, and the snaking letterforms (with the 'N's locked in their own pulse-like waveform) provided it. CNN's pictures of the attempted assassination of then president Ronald Reagan in 1981 soon got it noticed. In 1986, it was the only news channel that took NASA's feed of the seemingly routine launch of the doomed space shuttle Challenger. From then on, our view of the world's unforgettable news events – Tiananmen Square, the Gulf War, 9/11, the conflicts in Afghanistan and Iraq – has carried CNN's logo in the bottom-right corner.

02/Abacus
Publishing imprint, UK.
Designed by Unreal,
2006

03/KDDI
Telecoms operator,
Japan. Designed by
Bravis International,
2000
A view of earth
characterizes this
logo for Japan's
second-largest
telecoms business.

04/Way Out Associates
CCTV systems
consultancy, UK.
Designed by Crescent
Lodge, 2004
Mapping a path from A
to B (or 'W' to 'T') within
a fixed area, the logo
is a record of the route
taken, like that captured
by CCTV cameras.

05/Venise
Advertising agency,
France. Designed by
Coast, 2005

06/Film London
Strategic agency for
film and media, UK.
Designed by Arthur-
SteenHorneAdamson
(D: Marksteen Adamson,
Scott McGuffie), 2005
Spooling film and the
River Thames are both
conveyed in a single
fluid line.

07/Sidetrack Films
Film production
company, USA.
Designed by
Area 17, 2006

01/

02/

03/

01/Chieko Mori
Traditional koto player
and dancer, Japan.
Designed by Emmi
Salonen, 2006

02/East Dulwich Deli
Delicatessen, UK.
Designed by
Multistorey, 2001
A return to traditional,
ornamented, pre-
supermarket design for
this high quality food
store in south London.
Stationery is printed on
luxurious tinted paper
made from recycled
dollar notes.

03/Cinise
Chinese in-store
promotion, Japan.
Designed by Marvin,
2006
Daimaru department
stores wanted to
promote the theme
of 'modern Chinese'.

04/Kaleidofon
Norwegian music
information centre,
Norway. Designed by
Grandpeople, 2006

**05/Detroit Symphony
Orchestra**
Musical institution, USA.
Designed by Pentagram
(D: Paula Scher), 2000
The restoration of the
DSO's pre-war home, the
ornate Detroit Orchestra
Hall (a National Historic
Landmark), became the
natural starting point
for this identity, which
serves the orchestra,
the hall and its recently
added performing-
arts centre.

20

Typographic elements

'Typographic elements' collects logos based on the building blocks of the written language – letters of the alphabet, numerals, punctuation marks and symbols used in text.

The A–Z section offers a sense of the chameleon-like personalities of letters, as well as their potential as symbols. Each one can be redrawn and recomposed a myriad different ways. The shapes, symmetries and details contained within just a single letter, when it is set in alternative typefaces, present designers with a plentiful supply of possible starting points. Dots, tails, ascenders, descenders, serifs, ligatures and the negative space inside letters, when adapted, can all trigger new and interesting associations.

Naturally, not all are equal in the alphabetic beauty parade. Some upper- and lower-case letterforms score more highly than others in their mark-making possibilities. The popularity of certain letters in logo-making may simply be a reflection of the incidence of those letters in the language in question – 'K' is more common in German and Dutch than in English, for example – but how some designers must rub their hands when they are presented with a client whose name starts with an 'A' or an 'F', a 'G' or an 'M'.

Playing with punctuation marks, accents and text symbols seems to be a European pastime with roots that lie in the printing and typographic traditions of Germany, Italy, France and the UK. Professions drawn to specific marks in this field include PR and branding agencies, whose favourites are exclamation and quotation marks, and accountancy firms, who seem to like the precision and economy of a full stop.

1.20 Single
letters: A

01/

Azman
Architects

02/

03/

CAMBRIDGE ASSESSMENT

Scottish
Arts Council

04/

05/

06/

achmea

07/

08/

09/

01/Alliance Abroad Group
International internship and student volunteer programme, USA. Designed by Marc English Design, 2002

02/Azman Architects
Architecture practice, UK. Designed by Spin, 2004
Structurally sound letterforms ('aa') display the 'modernism with a twist' of Ferhan Azman.

03/Alliance of Artists' Communities
Support service for artist-in-residence programmes, USA. Designed by Malcolm Grear Designers, 2002
Two 'a's and a 'c', to be exact.

04/Cambridge Assessment
Educational assessment agency, UK. Designed by Spencer du Bois (D: John Spencer), 2005
Two good marks: an 'A' and a tick.

05/Scottish Arts Council
Funding, development and advocacy council for the arts, UK. Designed by Graven Images, 2002
Eagle-eyed design watchers spotted that the new logo revealed by QuarkXPress, makers of design software, in September 2005 was almost identical to that of the SAC. The software house was forced back to the drawing board.

06/Advance
In-house training programme, UK. Designed by Mytton Williams (D: Bob Mytton), 2003
One of the UK's largest providers of professional support services, Capita set up this internal training scheme.

07/Angel Arts Filmprojects
Film and video production agency, The Netherlands. Designed by smel, 2006

08/Achmea
Insurance provider, The Netherlands. Designed by Tel Design (D: Jaco Emmen, Eugene Heijblom), 2001

09/LG Arts Center
Cultural venue, South Korea. Designed by Lance Wyman, 1999
Flying the flag for the performing arts at a new state-of-the-art complex.

schouwburg **almere**

the national archives

アットローン

atina

10/Alcoa
Aluminium producer, USA
Designed by Saul Bass, 1963; updated by
Arnold Saks Associates, 1998
How many aluminium companies do you know
with a range of clothes and accessories bearing
their logo? In its stark geometric simplicity – and
resemblance to a stealth bomber – Alcoa's
emblem looks like it was designed yesterday.
The original, which was almost identical to this
'modernized' version save for a fuller 'A' inside
the rounded square, was created by Saul Bass in
1963. It followed the most celebrated phase of the
designer's career, in which he single-handedly
invented film titles for Otto Preminger, Billy
Wilder and Stanley Kubrick, as well as for Alfred
Hitchcock's 'Vertigo', 'North By Northwest' and
'Psycho'. Bass made an art out of defining movies
with a single enduring image and did the same for
a string of multinational corporations, including
AT&T, Minolta, United Airlines, Continental Airlines
and Alcoa.

11/Schouwburg Almere
Theatre, The
Netherlands. Designed
by ankerxstrijbos, 2006

**12/Pecoraro, Abrate,
Brunazzi & Associati**
Architecture studio,
Italy. Designed by
Brunazzi & Associati (D:
Andrea Brunazzi), 1999

**13/Attleboro Arts
Museum**
Community-based
museum, USA. Designed
by Malcolm Grear
Designers, 2004

14/The National Archives
Government records
agency, UK. Designed
by Spencer du Bois
(D: John Spencer), 2004

15/At-Loan
Financial services,
Japan. Designed by
Bravis International,
2004
More reminiscent of the
Coca Cola mark than a
bank, especially when
printed in red, this logo
is for the consumer
finance arm of the huge
Sumitomo Mitsui Banking
Corporation.

16/Átina
Supplier of natural anti-
inflammatory agents,
Brazil. Designed by
FutureBrand BC&H, 2004
Átina obtains alpha
bisabolol for use
in cosmetics and
pharmaceuticals, using
sustainable methods to
source the raw material
from candeia trees.

1.20 Single
letters: B

01/

02/

03/

04/

05/

06/

07/

TM

01/Bouwfonds
Property finance and development agency. The Netherlands. Designed by Total Identity (SD: André Mol), 2002
A 3D 'b' built from the ground up.

02/River Bluff Architecture
Architecture practice, USA. Designed by Design Ranch (AD, D: Michelle Sonderegger, Ingred Sidie), 2003

03/Bradford 2008
Capital of Culture programme, UK. Designed by Elmwood Recalling the 'joiner' style of photography developed by Bradford's son, David Hockney, the mark hints at the city's cultural and ethnic diversity.

04/Cartiere Burgo
Paper manufacturer, Italy. Designed by Brunazzi & Associati (D: Andrea Brunazzi), 2002

05/Bernard's
Gourmet market and café, USA. Designed by Eric Baker Design (CD: Eric Baker; D: Eric Strohl), 2003

06/St Barnabas House
Palliative care hospice, UK. Designed by Conran Design Group (D: Nicola Gray, Jonathan Coleman), 2006

07/ Wirtschaftsministerium Brandenburg
Regional ministry of economics, Germany. Designed by Thomas Manss & Company, 1996 Brandenburg's campaign to attract inward investment uses a forward-looking letter.

08/Bite
Advertising agency, UK. Designed by Blast, 1996 A partnership between a writer and an art director designed to leave an impression on clients.

09/Bongorama Productions
Event organizers, Denmark. Designed by A2/SW/HK, 2005

10/Badger Meter
Flow metering devices, USA. Designed by Crosby Associates, 1969

11/Beyon
Office furniture supplier, UK. Designed by SEA, 2001
A nice place to put your b-hind.

**1.20 Single
letters: C**

omroep voor kunst en cultuur

01/

02/

03/

04/

05/

FISH CENTRAL

Founded 1968

06/ .... 07/ .... 08/ ....

09/ ....

01/C
Arts-oriented
broadcaster, The
Netherlands. Designed
by Studio Dumbar, 2006
Different typographic
takes on the same letter
are combined to create
a single shape that
represents the multiple
points of view that
works of art and culture
typically generate.

02/Compass Centre
City University's
centre for speech and
language therapies, UK.
Designed by Crescent
Lodge, 2002

03/Chubb Corporation
Insurance group, USA.
Designer unknown

04/Corus
International metals
business, UK/The
Netherlands. Designed
by Enterprise IG, 1999
The merger of British
Steel and Koninklijke
Hoogovens demanded
a new name to herald
a single unified
business. The negative
space of the 'c' could
be an accompanying
trumpet or an allusion
to extrusion.

05/Central
Mixed-use development,
Singapore. Designed by
Fitch, 2005
Mimicking the copyright
symbol, the design
suggests uniqueness in
Far East Organization's
development of
apartments and shops
on the Singapore River.

06/Fish Central
Restaurant, UK.
Designed by Atelier
Works, 2003
A fish and chip shop
that went upmarket,
Fish Central needed
a logo that would look
good on china without
alienating its long-
standing local clientele.

07/Charmant Group
Eyewear brand, Japan.
Designed by Katsuichi
Ito Design Studio, 1995
A 'C' that sees.

**08/Commission for Rural
Communities**
Advisory body, UK.
Designed by Mytton
Williams (D: Bob Mytton,
Matt Judge), 2005
References to rustic
idylls, farming and
nature were not an
option for this
Cheltenham-based
organization that was
established to provide a
voice for disadvantaged
rural communities in
England.

**09/Centro de
Convenciones de
Cartagena**
Convention centre,
Colombia. Designed
by Chermayeff &
Geismar Inc. (D: Steff
Geissbuhler), 1981
Three 'c's on the open
sea: the centre is
located on the quayside
in the historic Caribbean
port of Cartagena.

1.20 Single
letters: D, E

01/

02/

03/

01/Daia Keiko
Fluorescent lighting manufacturer, Japan. Designed by Katsuichi Ito Design Studio, 2001

02/Datatrain
Software and training for facility managers and property owners, Germany. Designed by Thomas Manss & Company, 2004
A reversed-out cropped 'd' that hints at floor plans.

03/Electrolux
White goods manufacturer, Sweden. Designed by Carlo Vivarelli, 1962
As the market for domestic appliances boomed in the late 1950s, demand for Elektrolux's products grew abroad. It changed its name to the more universal Electrolux and held a contest across Scandinavia to find a design for a new corporate symbol to replace its tired-looking globe. For trademark-protection reasons, one condition was that the logo should include a globe. The results were disappointing, so the contest was taken to Switzerland, which had

a higher concentration of reductive, fiercely modernist designers and typographers than anywhere else in Europe. The winner was Carlo Vivarelli, whose entry, 'Sun/globe concave/convex', conflated the globe with an 'E' and gave Electrolux a symbol that soon became synonymous with kitchens, cleanliness and efficiency.

04/Earproof
Ear protection solutions, The Netherlands. Designed by The Stone Twins, 2005

05/Dell E-Business
E-commerce division, USA. Designed by Design Ranch, 2003

06/e-creators
Website developers, Japan. Designed by Taste Inc (D: Toshiyasu Nanbu), 2003

07/Eurostar
International railway, UK, France, Belgium. Designed by Minale Tattersfield (AD: Philippe Rasquinet, Jim Waters), 1994
Three European railways unified in a single letterform.

1.20 Single
letters: F

01/

02/

03/

04/

05/

06/

07/

08/

09/

10/

11/

01/Fidelity Life Association
Life insurance underwriter, USA. Designed by Crosby Associates, 2005

02/Folio Wines & Spirits
Fine wine merchant, UK. Designed by HGV, 2002 A logo of good character for the company formed when two respected wine merchants merged.

03/Facis
Men's fashion label, Italy. Designed by Brunazzi & Associati (D: Giovanni Brunazzi), 1999

04/Fusions
National association of clay and glass artists, Australia. Designed by Inkahoots, 2006

05/Fisher Scientific International Inc.
Scientific instruments and laboratory equipment, USA. Designed by Arnold Saks Associates, 1995

06/Fanfare for the Future
Royal Albert Hall's annual fundraising performance, UK. Designed by Hat-Trick Design, 2003 Every year a gala performance is staged to raise money for the hall's refurbishment. Its logo combines musical notation with one of the key tools of the restoration, and conjures up the title.

07/Fifth Town Artisan Cheese Co
Cheese-maker, Canada. Designed by Hambly & Woolley (CD: Bob Hambly; DD: Barb Woolley; D: Dominic Ayre), 2004 Mixing modern type with old-world sensitivities, the logo gives the impression that the company is well established in a region with an emerging food and wine industry.

08/Foresight Venture Partners
Hedge fund, UK. Designed by Johnson Banks, 2005

09/Danny Ferrington
Guitar maker, USA. Designed by Malcolm Grear Designers, 1978

10/Farmhouse Web
Web technology, USA. Designed by Templin Brink Design (CD: Joel Templin, Gaby Brink; D: Brian Gunderson), 1999

11/Fashion Center
New York business district, USA. Designed by Pentagram (D: Michael Bierut), 1993 The Garment District in mid-Manhattan, home to tailors, wholesalers and fashion houses, felt a bit fuzzy and anonymous. What went on there was strictly behind-the-scenes, if not top secret. Its edges were blurred: it was the only Business Improvement District on the island not based on a geographic area (such as Lower Manhattan or Columbus Avenue). The creation of a five-hole black button for the area that would now be called the Fashion Center – applied to advertising, streetlight banners, rubbish bins and in giant 3D at a landmark information kiosk – brought the area out of its shell.

GABI SZABO

01/

Greenwich Park
BAR & GRILL

02/

GENTICA
UNITED FOR ROMANIA

03/

04/

GROWTH
MATTERS

05/

06/

GRAVIS

07/

GENERAL MILLS

08/

09/

10/

Gilbert Collection

11/

01/Gabi Szabo
Celebrity, Romania.
Designed by Brandient,
2005
Former 5000m Olympic
champion Gabriela
Szabo needed a logo
for her post-retirement
celebrity status. The
stylized 'G' has been
extracted from her
signature.

**02/Greenwich Park
Bar & Grill**
Restaurant and bar, UK.
Designed by SomeOne
(D: Simon Manchipp,
David Law and Laura
Hussey), 2005

03/Gentica
Pan-EU lobby group of
expatriate Romanians.
Designed by Brandient,
2006
An association
established to promote
Romania's case for
accession and
integration within
the EU.

04/Greenwing
Honda motorcycle
dealerships, Thailand.
Designed by Chermayeff
& Geismar Inc. (D: Steff
Geissbuhler), 2005.
Motorcycle sales
with an 'eco-friendly
philosophy'.

05/Growth Matters
Business consultancy,
UK. Designed by
Crescent Lodge, 2003
As a corporate acronym
for a new business,
GM is worth avoiding.
Turning the 'm' into a
'3' alludes to the firm's
three areas of expertise
– business development,
communications and
marketing – and, as a
symbol ('to the power of
3'), suggests astonishing
rates of growth.

**06/Kyoto Gakuen
University**
University, Japan.
Designed by
Kokokumaru
(D: Yoshimaru
Takahashi), 1998

07/Gravis
PC sales and
distribution, Germany.
Designed by United
Designers Network

**08/The Gunmakers'
Charitable Trust**
Educational charity,
UK. Designed by Atelier
Works, 2005
Run by the Gunmakers'
Company, one of
the City of London's
historic Guilds, this trust
supports educational
scholarships and
bursaries. A small
addition to the 'g'
gives it firepower.

09/Grandpeople
Graphic design studio,
Norway. Designed by
Grandpeople, 2006

10/General Mills
Packaged foods group,
USA. Designed by
Lippincott Mercer, 1955
An extravagant 'g' with
curlicues, but there
might be an 'M' or
even a sack of flour
in there, too.

11/Gilbert Collection
Museum of decorative
arts, UK. Designed by
Atelier Works, 2000
On display at Somerset
House in London since
2000, the Gilbert
Collection is a £90-
million bequest of
jewelry and decorative
arts. This logo launched
the display; based on
an engraved snuffbox
design, it shows the
monogram of the
founder, Sir Arthur
Gilbert.

1.20 Single
letters: H

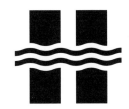

02/

03/

04/

05/

06/

07/

01/Hostage UK
Hostage-support charity, UK
Designed by Crescent Lodge, 2003
No one knows more about the experience of being taken and held hostage and its effects on one's family than Terry Waite. In the early 1980s, while acting as a special envoy of the Archbishop of Canterbury, Waite negotiated the release of a number of British hostages held in Iran and Libya. Then, while mediating with kidnappers in the Lebanon, Waite himself was taken captive and held for 1,763 days, the first four years of which were spent in solitary confinement. In 2005, he set up Hostage UK to counsel and support kidnap victims and their loved ones. Both groups are familiar with the marking of time as an attempt to gain a degree of control over a situation. Chalk marks on a wall give some sense of the solitude and helplessness felt by victims, and rendering the letter 'H' in the same way in the logo makes a powerful visual statement.

02/Honda
Engineering corporation, Japan. Designer unknown

03/South Waterfront Park, Hoboken
City of Hoboken, USA. Designed by Lance Wyman, 1995

04/Heritage Trails
Walking tours in Lower Manhattan, USA. Designed by Chermayeff & Geismar Inc. (D: Keith Helmetag), 1998

05/Hush
Garden design company, UK. Designed by Purpose, 2005

06/Hilton
Hotel group, USA. Designed by Enterprise IG
A mark to signify the unification of two separately owned brands: Hilton Hotels Corp and Hilton International.

07/Horstonbridge
Property development consultancy, UK. Designed by Brownjohn (D: James Beveridge, Andy Mosley), 2004
The logo reflects the company's claim to bridge the gap between delivering new developments and managing them.

i

01/

 INDESIT

02/

03/

Jade Jagger for **yoo**

01/DigitalScape
Recruitment agency for digital designers, Japan. Designed by Bravis International, 2003
Tweaking an 'i' to resemble 'hito', the Japanese character for 'person', puts the emphasis on the qualities of the individual.

02/Indesit
White goods manufacturer, Italy. Designed by Wolff Olins, 1998
Part of a pan-European repositioning of Indesit involved a shift in its marketing focus away from products and toward the consumer. The new identity was designed to convey youthfulness, affordability and simplicity.

03/Irwin Financial
Specialized financial services group, USA. Designed by Chermayeff & Geismar Inc. (D: Steff Geissbuhler), 1999

04/PGRDi
Pfizer Global Research & Development's informatics division, USA. Designed by Enterprise IG (CD: Will Ayres; DD: Dennis Thomas), 2004

05/Jade Jagger for Yoo
Identity for a creative director, UK. Designed by SomeOne (D: Laura Hussey, David Law, Simon Manchipp), 2007
An identity for Jade Jagger in her role as a creative director of Yoo, the property development firm of designer Philippe Starck and Manhattan Loft Company founder John Hitchcox. Jagger is 'interior stylist' of Yoo's developments; her logo, composed of fine interlinked 'J's, is intended to reflect her 'flowing and organic' design style.

1.20 Single
letters: K, L

kalideen
acu—
puncture

01/

02/

kelten römer museum manching

03/

04/

05/

06/

07/

08/

09/

10/

11/

01/Shereen Kalideen Acupuncture
Acupuncturist, UK. Designed by DA Design, 2006

02/Kentucky Music Hall of Fame & Museum
Exhibition about the musical heritage of Kentucky, USA. Designed by Malcolm Grear Designers, 1999

03/Kelten Römer Museum Manching
Celtic-Roman museum, Germany. Designed by Büro für Gestaltung Wangler & Abele, 2006 This museum, endeavouring to handle history in a modern open way, is housed in a building of Miesian lines and planes, and is symbolized by the lower-case sans-serif type and surprising composition.

04/Plaza Kinta
Shopping mall, Mexico. Designed by Lance Wyman, 1993

05/Klett Verlag
Educational publisher, Germany. Designed by MetaDesign, 2004 Familiar to generations of German school children, the logo features the initials of the founder, Ernst Klett, in the shape of a lily.

06/Kmart
Warehouse store chain, USA. Designed by G2 Branding & Design, 2004 A new look that accompanied Kmart's reorganization following its filing for Chapter 11 bankruptcy in 2002.

07/Kunstuitleen Utrecht
Art libraries, The Netherlands. Designed by ankerxstrijbos, 2005 K = kunst = art.

08/Lehner WerkMetall
Lighting manufacturer, Germany. Designed by Büro für Gestaltung Wangler & Abele and Eberhard Stauß, 2006 For Ursula Wangler and Frank Abele less is more. 'L' is not just a letter; as a right-angled form, it is the perfect way to convey the craftsmanship of traditional metalworking that is inherent in Lehner's custom-made architectural lighting systems.

09/Larry Ladig Photography
Advertising photographer, USA. Designed by Lodge Design (D: Eric Kass), 2006

10/Little Label
Record label, Norway. Designed by Kallegraphics, 2004

11/Lexus
Car maker, Japan. Designed by Siegel & Gale, 2002 The mark is part of a campaign by the luxury car brand to 'create a deeper emotional connection with its customers'.

1.20 Single
letters: M

01/

02/

03/

04/

05/

01/Message
Abbey Baptist Church
internal newspaper,
UK. Designed by Sam
Dallyn, 2001

02/Muzak
Music, messaging and
sound systems for
business, USA. Designed
by Pentagram (CD: Kit
Hinrichs), 1997
Muzak isn't just what
we call elevator music;
it's the company that
invented it. It was
founded in the 1930s to
provide music for typing
pools, and its recordings
were soon calming
anxious lift users in the
new skyscrapers of
American cities.

03/Mopar
Spare parts and service
for DaimlerChrysler's
brands, USA. Designed
1964
This firm's name is a
contraction of 'motor
parts'.

04/Metamorphosis
Personal image
consultancy, UK.
Designed by Thomas
Manss & Company, 1996
A caterpillar awaiting
transformation?

05/Marathon Consulting
IT consultancy, USA.
Designed by Area 17,
2006
An attempt to position
IT, as practised by
this firm, as 'a high-
performance sport', with
references to a pulse
and a mountain range.

06/Mexico City Metro
Metro system, Mexico.
Designed by Lance
Wyman, 1968
Almost single-handedly,
Lance Wyman crafted
a new, modern,
outward-looking identity
for Mexico in the late
1960s. Not only did
the world witness his
reverberating graphics
for the 1968 Olympic
Games, but it also saw
his identity system
for Mexico City's new
metro network, the first
in the world to include
individual symbols
for each station that
related to the name of
the stop or the history
of the area around it.
For 40 years, these have
helped non-Spanish-
speaking visitors
navigate a vast city.

07/Motorclean
Car valeting company,
UK. Designed by Glazer,
2006

M Flughafen München

08/

WARREN M MILLER

09/

10/

11/

HermanMiller

13/   14/   15/

16/

08/Flughafen München
International airport, Germany. Designed by Otl Aicher and Eberhard Stauß, 1992; updated by Büro für Gestaltung Wangler & Abele, 2001
Aicher, who was also responsible for the Lufthansa identity in 1969, and Stauß created the unique 'M' when the airport opened. Today, three of the letters, each 12m high, greet visitors on the access road to the airport.

09/Middlesex Probation Service
Probation service, UK. Designed by Johnson Banks, 1995
Neither prison nor community service, successful probation is all about going straight.

10/Warren Miller
Action-sports filmmaker, USA. Designed by Templin Brink Design (CD: Joel Templin, Gaby Brink; D: Paul Howalt), 1998
Doubling as snowy peaks, the 'M' is for a maker of extreme ski and snowboard films.

11/Media Rights
Non-profit distributor of social issue films, USA. Designed by Open, 2000

12/Mushroom Records
Record label, Australia. Designed by Frost Design (D: Vince Frost, Anthony Donovan), 2005
Following Mushroom's sale to Warner Music Australia, this look was created to preserve the image of independence.

13/Herman Miller
Furniture manufacturer, USA. Designed by Irving Harper, 1947
Harper, working in the studio of HM's design director George Nelson in 1947, devised the logo when asked to create a press advertisement for a new line of furniture. Without any photographs of the new designs to work from, he fashioned his own two-dimensional, wood-grain piece of furniture from the 'M' of Miller. He continued to apply the emblem in subsequent ads, refining it as he went along, until it was permanently adopted by the company. There is such a thing as a free logo.

14/Musées de France
Public museums, France. Designed by Studio Apeloig, 2005
Designed for the Ministry of Culture, this 'appellation' is for French state-owned museums that have public access.

15/Meubles.com
Online furniture retailer, France. Designed by FL@33 (D: Agathe Jacquillat, Tomi Vollauschek), 2004

16/McDonalds
Fast-food restaurants, USA. Designed by Jim Schindler, 1962
When Ray Kroc started franchising Dick and Mac McDonald's walk-up hamburger stands in 1955, the standard building design included a pair of streamlined arches, one on each side of the stand. On approaching the stand from an angle, the arches formed a golden 'M', which later became the basis for the chain's logo.

**1.20 Single
letters: N, O**

01/

02/

03/

01/Novensys
Information
management systems,
Romania. Designed by
Brandient (Cristian
Petre), 2004
A new name and identity
for a Bucharest business
that had grown rapidly
since it started as BCS
Romania, a provider
of bar-code systems,
in 1995.

02/Nicola Tilling
Freelance marketing
specialist, UK. Designed
by Mytton Williams
(D: Bob Mytton, Gary
Martyniak), 2006
On charts and graphs,
an 'N' always ends on
an up.

**03/Oval Innovation
Japan**
Educational non-profit
organization, Japan.
Designed by Shinnoske
Inc (AD: Shinnoske
Sugisaki; D: Ami
Okamoto), 2006
OIJ works to encourage
the development of
new universities in
local areas. The mark
represents a flexible
and responsive
organization.

04/Oxiteno
Chemical producer,
Brazil. Designed by
FutureBrand BC&H, 2005

05/Sydney Olympic Park
Olympic Games venue,
Australia. Designed by
Saatchi Design, 2002

1.20 Single
letters: P, Q

PLUSUN

01/

PARK
SQUARE

02/

03/

01/Plusun Corporation
Mobile Internet systems
corporation, Japan.
Designed by Taste Inc
(D: Toshiyasu Nanbu),
2003

02/Park Square
Calthorpe Estates
property development,
UK. Designed by
Brownjohn (D: James
Beveridge, Andy
Mosley), 2006

03/PressWatch Media
Press cuttings and
media analysis agency,
UK. Designed by Blast,
2004.
Scanning the press,
wires and Web for
coverage of their clients.

04/Quality Foodcare
Specialist catering for
hospitals, UK. Designed
by Atelier Works, 1996
Meals that get finished,
and a logo that went
down well.

05/Quark
Desktop-publishing
and graphic-design
software, USA. Designed
by Quark, 2006
Six months after its new
identity was accused
of bearing too close a
resemblance to that of
the Scottish Arts Council
(see p. 97), Quark
launched a different
logo, designed by
their internal creative
team rather than
by consultants, that
was unquestionably,
unequivocally a 'Q'.

1.20 Single
letters: R, S

01/

REARDEN
commerce

02/

03/

04/

05/

SIGMAX

06/

sciencon

07/

01/Cherry R
Art gallery, Japan.
Designed by
Kokokumaru
(D: Yoshimaru
Takahashi), 2003

02/Rearden Commerce
E-commerce platform,
USA. Designed by
Templin Brink Design
(CD: Joel Templin,
Gaby Brink; D: Gaby
Brink), 2004

03/Rakunan Car Co.
Car dealership, Japan.
Designed by
Kokokumaru
(D: Yoshimaru
Takahashi), 1997

**04/Sonesta
International Hotels**
International hotel
chain, USA. Designed
by Malcolm Grear
Designers, 1979

**05/Stockwell
Partnership**
Urban regeneration
initiative, UK. Designed
by Atelier Works, 2003
This alliance between
local businesses,
community groups
and residents in the
south London ward of
Stockwell was formed
to channel government
funding into local urban
improvement schemes.

06/Sigmax
Medical and sports aids,
Japan. Designed by
Taste Inc (D: Toshiyasu
Nanbu), 2005

07/Sciencon
Welding consultancy,
Sweden. Designed by
Sam Dallyn, 2003
Sciencon specializes in
technical welding for
next-generation energy
installations.

08/Superga
Shoes and sportswear
producer, Italy.
Designed by Brunazzi &
Associati (D: Giovanni
Brunazzi), 1999

09/STV
Regional TV channel,
UK. Designed by
Elmwood, 2006
Two stations – Scottish
TV and Grampian TV
– were rebranded as
one by SMG Television.

10/Statkraft
Electricity supplier,
Norway. Designed 1992
Statkraft began life in
1992 when Norway's
state-owned power
supplier was privatized.
Light and dark, yin
and yang: an 'S' in
a circle can suggest
many things.

11/Seat
Car manufacturer,
Spain. Designed by
Enterprise IG
Founded as a subsidiary
of Fiat in 1950, Seat
is now owned by the
Volkswagen Group. The
acronym Seat stood for
Sociedad Española de
Automóviles de Turismo
(Spanish Touring Car
Corporation). Under
VW's wing, Seat is
modernizing and going
after international
markets. The striped 'S'
logo is based on the first
letter of the company's
previous logotype.

1.20 Single
letters: T, U, V

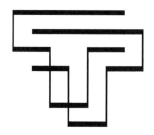

01/

02/

03/

04/

05/

01/Twins Foundation
Non-profit information centre on twins and other multiples, USA. Designed by Malcolm Grear Designers, 1983

02/Telemundo
Spanish-language TV network, USA. Designed by Chermayeff & Geismar Inc. (D: Steff Geissbuhler, Robert Matza), 1992

03/Trinity Repertory
Theatre company, USA. Designed by Malcolm Grear Designers, 2000

04/Aveny-T
Theatre, Denmark. Designed by A2/SW/HK, 2001

05/Transitions
Radio show, tour and album series, UK. Designed by Malone Design (D: David Malone, Nick Tweedie), 2005
Implying continuous change, the Möbius strip mark was developed as a brand for DJ John Digweed's musical enterprises.

06/Ursem
Construction group, The Netherlands. Designed by Total Identity (D: Aad van Dommelen, Jeanette Kaptein), 2004

07/United Airlines
International airline, USA. Designed by Saul Bass & Associates, 1973; modified by Pentagram, 1997, and Fallon Worldwide, 2004
Despite tinkering with the logotype over the years – adding 'Airlines' then removing it, moving to a serif font and back again – United has stuck by Saul Bass's 'double U' symbol.

08/Univision
Spanish-language TV network, USA. Designed by Chermayeff & Geismar Inc. (D: Tom Geismar, Steff Geissbuhler), 1989

09/Votorantim
Industrial conglomerate, Brazil. Designed by FutureBrand BC&H, 1999

10/Vanderbilt University
University, USA. Designed by Malcolm Grear Designers, 2001
Vanderbilt's established oak-leaf-and-acorn symbolism is given a new expression.

11/Hotel Velta
Hotel, Japan. Designed by Kokokumaru (D: Yoshimaru Takahashi), 2005

WEDGWOOD

ENGLAND 1759

01/

Westinghouse

02/

03/

04/

WEDNESDAYITE

WalkerInformation

WILMORITE
CONSTRUCTION

05/   06/   07/

01/Wedgwood
Fine-china producer, UK. Designed by The Partners (AD: Aziz Cami, Nina Jenkins; D: Steve Owen, Tony De Ste Croix), 2000

02/Westinghouse
Electrical appliance manufacturing group, USA. Designed by Paul Rand, 1960
When Rand presented this logo to the Westinghouse board, whose members were accustomed to the heavy antique emblem by their company patriarch George Westinghouse, there was a dumbfounded silence followed by a discontented murmur. It was likened to a crown, a pawnbroker's balls and a cartoon character. Only after an intervention by Rand's champion and the company's design director, Eliot Noyes, was the design accepted. It became a landmark logo in the branding of heavyweight industrial companies. Despite the late 1990s break-up of the old Westinghouse, the logo is still used by the consumer electrical and nuclear power businesses that bear the name under new ownership.

03/The Wheeler School
Independent day school, USA. Designed by Malcolm Grear Designers, 2004
Founded in 1889 by Mary Colman Wheeler, an American Impressionist painter and educator, this nursery and coeducational school is on Rhode Island.

04/Wilberforce
Slave trade abolition bicentenary identity, UK. Designed by Elmwood, 2005
In 1807 William Wilberforce's campaign to abolish the slave trade was finally rewarded. Leading the bicentennial celebrations was Wilberforce's birthplace, the city of Hull. To raise awareness of the anniversary and to promote Hull's renaissance beyond 2007, Hull City Image commissioned an identity that avoided clichéd images associated with slavery and looked more like a brand used by a human rights organization.

05/Wednesdayite
Football supporters' club, UK. Designed by Atelier Works, 2005
This mark is for the independent supporters' club of Sheffield Wednesday, who play in blue and white stripes.

06/Walker Information
Customer and stakeholder research consultancy, USA. Designed by Crosby Associates, 1995

07/Wilmorite Construction
Construction contractor, USA. Designed by Moon Brand (D: Peter Dean), 2001
Wilmorite, the shopping-centre developer, has a logo (also by Moon Brand) that comprises five coloured blocks assembled into a 'W'. For buildings still under construction, the designers came up with this skeletal version.

01/

02/

03/

X BY 2
Architecture First

Hotxt™

01/Xinet
Digital asset
management for
prepress and printing,
USA. Designed by
Pentagram (CD Brian
Jacobs; D: Julio
Martinex, Kit Hinrichs),
2006

02/Taleo
Executive talent
management agency,
USA. Designed by Addis
Creson, 2005
A team of talented
individuals is greater
than the sum of its parts.

03/X-Rite
Colour measurement
technology, USA.
Designed by BBK Studio,
2004
X marks the spot for a
business making high-
precision technology
for the printing, imaging
and medical industries.

04/X by 2
Technology consulting
group, USA. Designed by
BBK Studio, 2005
This group designs and
builds complex internal
business systems.

05/Hotxt
Text-messaging service,
UK. Designed by SEA,
2006.
A service that uses the
Internet to send text
messages between
members. The logo
is based on the
affectionate way
of signing off a
message: 'x'.

01/

02/

03/

K20 K21
KUNSTSAMMLUNG NORDRHEIN-WESTFALEN

WOOD ST

8:59
centrepoint
what's next for young people

04/

05/

06/

gm2

12move

07/

08/

09/

01/3
International mobile-phone network, UK. Designed by 3, 2002
Back in 2002, 3G (third-generation technology) was big news and the key to a whole world of wonderful new things on your mobile, like video telephony. So it was a coup for Hutchison Whampoa to be able to name its 3G service '3' – a name, a number and a logo. On top of that, it was memorable and transcended language. And, according to numerologists, it was even a lucky number.

02/More 4
Digital TV station, UK. Designed by Spin, 2005
The increasing size of the lozenges makes a '4' and suggests more.

03/T.26
Digital type foundry, USA. Designed by Segura Inc, 2005
Founded by Carlos Segura in 1994, the font shop has continually reinvented its own logo to reflect its ever-expanding library of fonts.

04/K20 K21
Museums of modern art, Germany. Designed by Claus Koch Corporate Communications, 2001
The opening of the second museum to display the acclaimed modern art collection of North Rhine-Westphalia necessitated a new joint identity that connected the two galleries but distinguished the two separate sites. 'K' stands for 'Kunst' (art), while the '20' and '21' refer to the centuries covered by each of the galleries.

05/1 Wood St
Property development, UK. Designed by Radford Wallis (CD, D: Stuart Radford, Andrew Wallis; D: Graham Birch), 2005
Wood Street is an office and retail development by Land Securities in the City of London.

06/Centrepoint
Charity for young homeless people, UK. Designed by Corporate Edge, 2003
Just before the working day begins in the UK, 8:59 is the moment of 'anticipation, potential and hope'. It was chosen as the symbol to represent Centrepoint's aim of offering young people the chance to find a better life.

07/gm2
Logistics for paper companies, UK. Designed by Roundel (D: Mike Denny), 2001
A company that moves paper of all weights (or grams per square metre, gm²) around the UK.

08/+15
Urban skywalk system, Canada. Designed by Lance Wyman, 1984
Roughly 15 feet above street level, +15 is a 16km-long pedestrian walkway that links dozens of downtown Calgary buildings via 59 enclosed bridges.

09/12Move
Internet service provider, The Netherlands. Designed by Total Identity, 1998

**Lulu
&Red.**

01/

DESIGN **PLUS**

Ebbsfleet
Valley

flisch¥
schifferli

02/   03/   04/

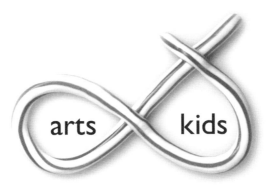

01/Lulu & Red
Independent fashion house, UK. Designed by Stylo Design (AD, D: Tom Lancaster), 2004
According to the brief from fashion designers Sarah Rees and Julian Dominique, the identity for this new womenswear label had to be friendly and incorporate a cat. A pair of judicious additions to the ampersand saved the day.

02/Design Plus
Design competition, Germany. Designed by Stankowski & Duschek, 1984
An award given for outstanding product design at the Ambiente international trade fair at the Messe Frankfurt.

03/Ebbsfleet Valley
Regeneration zone, UK. Designed by Hat-Trick, 2006
Plans for this 1000-acre regeneration area in Kent Thameside promise a lot: great housing and public spaces; outstanding infrastructure and transport connections; a sense of community and a commitment to sustainability. The '&' or 'E' stands for Ebbsfleet and the inclusiveness it claims to represent.

04/flisch + schifferli
Vineyard, Switzerland. Designed by Büro für Gestaltung Wangler & Abele, 2005
When two young vintners, Peter Flisch and Andrin Schifferli, took over a long-established Swiss vineyard, the emblem of the previous owners – an image of wine exploding from the top of a bottle – was reduced to a '+' sign to connect the two new names.

05/Mair Education
Educational advisor, UK. Designed by Funnel Creative, 2005
An identity for a sole practitioner, Sara Mair, that turns the 'E' into an ampersand to suggest 'Me and (you, the client)'.

06/Ampersand
Periodical, UK. Designed by Frost Design
'Ampersand' is the members' magazine produced by D&AD, the international association of creative practitioners in design and advertising.

07/Prince of Wales' Arts & Kids Foundation
Children's arts charity, UK. Designed by Atelier Works, 2003
Arts & Kids aims to inspire and educate children by funding events, performances and exhibitions around the UK. Its logo, drawn in a number of different media from graffiti to ribbon to toothpaste, reflects children's own innate creativity.

ÅHLÉNS

Architectural Education Trust

making opportunity equal in architecture.

comma

01/

02/

03/

Nåtiønàl Intérprẽtinğ Sërviçê

04/

05/

06/

07/

equator

Deloitte.

08/   09/   10/

Art Review:

11/

01/Åhléns
Department-store chain, Sweden. Designed by Stockholm Design Lab, 1997
Part of a modernization programme for Sweden's largest chain of department stores in the 1990s, this new identity lends a human character to the 'Å'.

02/Architectural Education Trust
Funding for architecture students, UK. Designed by NB: Studio (AD: Nick Finney, Ben Stott, Alan Dye), 2005

03/Comma
Internal communications consultancy, UK. Designed by HGV, 2006
Sometimes, a short pause in the right place can make a big difference.

04/National Interpreting Service
Over-the-phone translation service, UK. Designed by Browns, 2003
Subscribers to the NIS – mainly large corporations and public authorities – have 24-hour access to translators of 150 languages. That's a lot of accents.

05/Cito
Testing and assessment firm for education and training, The Netherlands. Designed by Tel Design (D: Jaco Emmen, René de Jong), 2005
An international firm of professional question-setters.

06/Inqira Consulting
Management consultancy, UK. Designed by Johnson Banks, 2005

07/Vodafone
Mobile-phone network operator, UK. Designed by Enterprise IG, 2005
Vodafone introduced its 'speech mark' identity in 1998. As well as the symbol, there used to be opening and closing quotation marks made from the negative space of the two 'o's in the name. The latest version lays greater emphasis on the symbol, giving it a more 3D form.

08/Equator
Plumbing system manufacturer, UK. Designed by Glazer, 2003
The '0°' refers to the name of a simple modern pipe system for central heating and to the temperature inside your home).

09/What's Next
Business intelligence reports, Australia. Designed by Layfield Design

10/Deloitte
Business consultancy, UK. Designed by Enterprise IG
Rather than separate its consulting and accountancy businesses, Deloitte & Touche wanted to bring them under a single 'master brand'. The '& Touche' was replaced by a full stop to 'represent the complete firm and the comprehensive nature of the Deloitte offer'.

11/Art Review
Arts magazine, UK. Designed by Spin, 2005
A colon introduces the reader to the contents.

!K.R.P.R

National
Museums
Scotland

"docfest"

12/

13/

14/

akademika"

15/

activ.mob.

16/

17/

18/

12/Katie Rosenberg Public Relations
Public-relations agency, USA. Designed by Thomas Manss & Company, 1996
Two of the PR trade's favourite tools are included here: an ellipsis and an exclamation mark.

13/National Museums Scotland
Umbrella organization for Scottish museums, UK. Designed by Hat-Trick, 2006
To raise awareness of a group of six museums, this brand incorporates a national flag composed of questions and answers.

14/Docfest
International documentary film festival, USA. Designed by Open, 1998
Docfest is an annual showcase of documentaries from around the world. The logo celebrates the fact that there are no scripts: the words in the films are taken from life.

15/Akademika
Chain of university bookshops, Norway. Designed by Mission Design, 2005

16/activ.mob.
Campaign to encourage exercise among the elderly, UK. Designed by Kent Lyons, 2005
The UK Design Council wanted to show how design can help combat chronic illnesses such as diabetes, back pain and arthritis by encouraging elderly people to seek regular exercise in groups, or 'mobs'. This logo forms the basis of a flexible identity system that groups can adapt themselves.

17/Newsgrade
Web-based financial news service, USA. Designed by Pentagram (D: Woody Pirtle), 2000

18/Blackpool Pleasure Beach
Amusement park, UK. Designed by Johnson Banks, 2006
'Brilliant!' The exclamatory reactions of the Pleasure Beach's seven-million visitors each year provided the starting point for the park's new logo.

19/Centre de Chant Choral de Namur
Classical singing centre, Belgium. Designed by Coast, 2005
A reversed speech mark or bubble indicates the oral nature of the music created and recorded at this centre.

20/The Climate Group
Emissions reduction coalition, UK. Designed by Browns, 2004
Established to mobilize support among corporations and governments for action on carbon dioxide emissions, The Climate Group is a non-profit organization that did not need a wishy-washy tree or earth eco-logo. Its identity captures the group's growing concern about global warming.

21/Greenberg
Brand marketing research agency, USA. Designed by Turner Duckworth (AD: David Turner, Bruce Duckworth; D: Shawn Rosenberger), 2003
Greenberg's 'questioning ear' suggests that the agency asks the right questions and listens closely to the answers.

22/Blaauboer United Vision
Trend research consultancy, The Netherlands. Designed by smel, 2004

23/

24/

25/

horizon.

26/

27/

28/

29/

Kseg.
ñocturnal groove
YELL.COM

MÜNSTER _____
_____
_KULTURHAUPTSTADT
FÜR_ EUROPA __ 2010

23/Swedish Institute
Agency promoting Sweden internationally, Sweden. Designed by BankerWessel (D: Ida Wessel), 2002

24/Public Radio International
International public radio station, USA. Designed by Pentagram (D: Michael Gericke), 1994

25/The Firm
Public-relations agency, UK. Designed by Radford Wallis (CD and D: Stuart Radford, Andrew Wallis), 2006

26/Horizon
Marketing and design consultancy, UK. Designed by NB: Studio (AD: Nick Finney, Ben Stott, Alan Dye), 2000

27/Breast Team
Medical team, Japan. Designed by Shinnoske Inc, 2003
With characters and bracket marks arranged to resemble a face, this identity for the Breast Team at Osaka Welfare Pension Hospital is intended to inspire confidence and approachability.

28/Sure Mobile
Mobile-phone service, UK. Designed by Conran Design Group (D: Richard Hood), 2006

29/Hagah
Media group, Brazil. Designed by FutureBrand BC&H, 2000

30/KSEG
Chartered accountants, UK. Designed by Kino Design, 2005

31/Nocturnal Groove
Record label, UK. Designed by Malone Design (D: David Malone), 2004
An umlaut above the 'n' is there as a pair of eyes to add personality, although a happier way of looking at it is as two people with their arms linked.

32/Yell.com
Local services search engine, UK. Designed by Johnson Banks, 2001
Inspiration for the dot, in the '.com', came from the yellow square that encloses the walking fingers of Yellow Pages' main logo.

33/Stadt Münster
Civic promotion, Germany. Designed by Claus Koch Corporate Communications, 2003
Münster's bid to be a European Capital of Culture in 2010 centres on the theme of correspondence. The flexible identity, for posters, literature and advertising, leaves space for citizens to add their own thoughts, words and images.

1.23 Punctuation
marks

35/   36/   37/

38/   39/   40/

34/(RED)
International fundraising brand coalition, UK
Designed by Wolff Olins, 2005
(RED) is the brainchild of Bono and the politician/
businessman/philanthropist Bobby Shriver. By
partnering with major consumer brands and
diverting part of their profits on certain products to
The Global Fund, (RED) hopes to raise awareness
and funds in the battle against the African AIDS
epidemic. The venture positions itself between the
worlds of business and philanthropy by presenting
a purchasing choice to consumers, rather than
appealing purely to their sense of charity. For its
identity, Wolff Olins recommended the creation of a
visual bond between the coalition and its partner
brands that would be closer and more unified than
the traditional co-branding solution of placing
two marks side-by-side. The choice of brackets
around logos such as those of American Express,
The Gap and Motorola, and the placement of 'RED'
in superscript, suggests an 'embrace' of partner
brands 'to the power of (RED)'. The colour red was
chosen to convey a sense of urgency and passion.
In its first six months, (RED) delivered an estimated
$25 million to the global fund.

35/ATP
National pension
scheme, Denmark.
Designed by
Kontrapunkt, 2003
Previously seen as
a bureaucratic and
dusty organization, ATP
adopted a new identity
that reflected its strong
performance – equal
to any private-sector
pension provider – and
the democratic ethos at
its heart.

36/Turner Duckworth
Branding and
packaging agency, UK
and USA. Designed by
Turner Duckworth

37/Control Finance
Recruitment agency for
financial professionals,
The Netherlands.
Designed by The Stone
Twins, 1999
An identity that has
nothing to do with
moving decimal points
around.

38/Tate Families
Campaign to increase
gallery access for
families, UK. Designed
by Rose, 2006

39/360 Architecture
Architecture and
interior design firm, USA.
Designed by Design
Ranch (AD: Michelle
Sonderegger, Ingred
Sidie; D: Michelle
Sonderegger), 2004

40/Elan
Manufacturer of
paint for building
professionals, France.
Designed by Area 17,
2005

Symbols

In this book, symbols refer to logos in which the principal message is conveyed through abstract shapes and patterns, signs (such as the arrow and the cross) or representational imagery.

The modern human mind has become incredibly adept at interpreting symbols. We are surrounded by this kind of visual shorthand: icons and isotype people on road signs, dashboards, computer screens and supermarket packaging, in magazines, maps and manuals. We are able to dissect symbols for meaning with laser precision. Shapes and images (squares, waves, leaves, globes and hearts, for example) carry unequivocal associations that form the common currency of logo design. Our minds are ravenous for meaning; given more ambiguous images, we cannot help but fill in the gaps in ways the creators never envisaged. We can see pictures within pictures, sometimes when they are not even there.

This speed of comprehension by an audience means that, in identity design, symbols perform quite different functions to logotypes and letters, and organizations have to make strategic decisions about which will serve them best. Wordmarks tend to be chosen in cases where the emphasis is on establishing name recognition – for a start-up company, perhaps, or one entering new markets – and where the name is distinctive and memorable (and short). Where words would be a handicap, either because a name is too long or does not translate well, a symbol has the advantage. Symbols can be designed to either loosen or reinforce a name's links with place and culture. As tribal emblems, they are popular with political organizations, fashion and sportswear companies and car manufacturers, not to mention employees. They can also provide a bottomless source of opening conversational gambits; like the cover of a good book, a great symbol usually has a great story attached.

Abstract

Some design watchers see the emergence of the abstract symbol in identity design as evidence of a poverty of ideas and of an inexorable slide towards sameness, propelled by myopic marketing departments. It is undoubtedly true that non-specific swirls, swooshes, whorls and waveforms have become the default option for organizations that cannot find anything interesting to say about themselves, but it would be wrong to write off the abstract logo.

There are degrees of abstraction, as this section readily shows, and at each level, memorable marks are possible. At one end of the scale, an element as simple as a square can become, in the hands of a designer of the genius of Anton Stankowski, the basis for striking creativity. Designs that appear to be non-representational occasionally have their origins in more figurative forms, Gepe's double-arrowhead and Bosch's lantern being good examples. Others might intimate real things: people can be reduced to dots, a piano keyboard to a few black bars, landscapes to contours. Less is more,

of course. A lone pair of black squares might not seem to offer much in the way of potent symbolism, except when they portray the footprints of the two towers of the World Trade Center.

More generally, squares and rectangles are employed for their ability to suggest stability, security and dependability, which is why banks and financial service firms like them. Mathematically derived forms and formations make pleasing representations of complexity, and are favoured by academic institutions, publishers and innovation-focused enterprises. Solid vertical bars make allusions that are relevant to businesses in the film, music and property arenas.

Included in this section are wordmarks enclosed within shapes, such as those for American Express, ABC and Pfizer, where the square, circle or oval is an integral and defining part of the design. There is also a handful that are not abstract – Shell and Hear US, for example – but which fit best into categories in this section.

The Chemical Company

Fraunhofer Gesellschaft

China
Heritage
Society

werk bund

09

01/BASF
Chemicals, Germany.
Designed by Interbrand
Zintzmeyer & Lux, 2003
Two complementary
squares, introduced to
what was previously
a type-only logo, are
intended to represent
a lock and key, or
'partnership and
collaboration to ensure
mutual success'. BASF
stands for Badische
Anilin & Sodafabrik and
was founded 1865.

02/Craftsteak
Restaurant at the MGM
Grand, USA. Designed
by Eric Baker Design
Associates (CD, D: Eric
Baker), 2003

**03/Fraunhofer-
Gesellschaft**
Alliance of applied
research institutes,
Germany. Designed by
Büro für Gestaltung
Wangler & Abele and
Eberhard Stauß, 1995

04/Birds Eye View
Theatre group, UK.
Designed by Spin, 2004

**05/Disasters Emergency
Committee**
National aid agencies'
umbrella organization,
UK. Designed by
Spencer du Bois
(D: John Spencer), 1997
Like the disaster-
stricken communities
supported by the DEC,
the square needs to be
put back on its feet.

**06/AMB Property
Corporation**
Industrial property
developer and owner,
USA. Designer unknown
A name built out of
the three co-founders'
surname initials and
a logo that suggests
a trio of substantial
properties.

07/400 ASA
Salah Benacer,
photographer, France.
Designed by Area 17,
2005

**08/China Heritage
Society**
Preservation and
promotion of traditional
Chinese crafts, France.
Designed by Rose, 2003
In traditional Chinese
architecture, structures
were built as a north-
to-south-oriented
walled compound,
with the main entrance
on the south side in
keeping with Feng Shui
principles.

09/Deutscher Werkbund
National association
of architects and
designers, Germany.
Designed by Stankowski
& Duschek, 1963
The first of three
logos in this section
by a giant of postwar
German graphic design,
Anton Stankowski, in
whose professional
commissions and art
the square was a
consistent theme.

10/

11/

12/

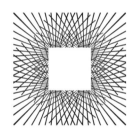 *The* **BANK** *of* **NEW YORK**

10/American Express
Travel, financial and
network services
provider, USA. Designed
by Lippincott Mercer,
1975

**11/WTC 9/11 Tribute
Center**
Ground Zero visitor
centre, USA. Designed
by Lance Wyman Ltd
and The Arnell Group
(D: Lance Wyman,
Peter Arnell), 2006
Two indelible footprints
in a unique relationship,
recalling an
unforgettable event.

12/B&Q
Home improvement and
garden centre retailer,
UK. Designed in 2002
Designed for high
visibility on a wide
range of applications,
the orange square was
also chosen for easy
modification to Far
Eastern markets. The
shape portrays 'space,
rooms and the home
in an abstract, but
adaptable format'.

**13/City University of
New York**
Urban university, USA.
Designer unknown
This stronger, more
solid presence replaced
an ageing house-like
pentagon logo.

14/Pongauer Holzbau
Traditional wooden
house builder, Austria.
Designed by Modelhart
Design, 2005
A building front, a sketch
or a wooden joint?

15/Marianne Strokirk
Hairdressing salon, USA.
Designed by Crosby
Associates, 1989

16/The Bank of New York
Financial services
group, USA. Designed by
Lippincott Mercer, 2005
After a period of
aggressive acquisition,
the Bank of New York
transformed itself from
a regional bank into a
global corporate and
institutional financial
services powerhouse.
The intricate patterns of
the bank's movements
of assets around the
world are symbolized
in its logo. The interior
white square denotes
a focus on its expertise
and experience.

20/

21/

22/

23/

17/Department of Culture, Media and Sport
British government department, UK.
Designed by CDT, 1999
A noble attempt to position the DCMS 'squarely at the centre of creative thought'.

18/Lego Group
Toy manufacturer, Denmark. Designed by DotZero (D: Rolf Lagerson), 1973; modified, 1998
Created at a time when 'bubble' lettering was de rigueur in the kids' market and when Lego was rapidly expanding internationally, this single emblem replaced the various logos that had been in use.

19/DLA
Legal services group, UK. Designed by CDT, 2003
Offering an alternative to the UK's 'magic circle' of legal practices, this law firm wanted to be seen as open-minded and down-to-earth, and therefore required a straight-talking, almost municipal, identity.

20/The Bond Market Association
Trade association for brokers and dealers, USA. Designed by Chermayeff & Geismar Inc. (D: Steff Geissbuhler), 1997
An appealing sight for those with an eye for rising values.

21/Museo de Arte Contemporáneo de Monterrey
Contemporary art museum, Mexico. Designed by Lance Wyman, 1990
In Spanish, 'marco' means 'frame'. Squares, in the windows, entrances and central courtyard, are the defining motif in Marco's warmly hued modernist building designed by Ricardo Legorreta.

22/Edward Jones
Investment services, USA. Designed by Crosby Associates, 1994

23/Lowe Advertising
International advertising agency group, UK. Designed by Carter Wong Tomlin, 2002
Briefed 'not to upset the horses', CWT ended up cutting the chairman's name in half. Square letterforms suggest the simplicity of an oriental woodcut – a highly visible mark in all media.

2.1 Squares

: EDINBURGH ART FESTIVAL

24/

25/

26/

27/

28/

D cube

24/Edinburgh Art Festival
Annual visual arts event, UK. Designed by Graphical House, 2005

25/Frankfurt Messe
Trade conference and exhibition venue, Germany. Designed by Stankowski & Duschek, 1983

26/Design Council
National design promotion agency, UK. Designed by Tayburn, 1996
A picture of stability and confidence painted in the wake of the root-and-branch reform of the Design Council in the mid-1990s.

27/ZDNet
Online business technology forum, USA. Designer unknown

28/Orange
Mobile phone operator, UK. Designed by Wolff Olins, 1994
Orange's name, colour, logo, identity system and tone confounded the grey unfriendly mobile phone industry of the early 1990s.

29/Villa Stuck
Museum, Germany. Designed by KMS Team (D: Knut Maierhofer), 1993
Former home of painter Franz von Stuck, the art nouveau building is now a museum.

30/Dcube
Website design and consultancy, Japan. Designed by Taste Inc, 2006

31/Media Trust
Non-profit communications support for voluntary organizations, UK. Designed by Form, 2006

32/SAS Scandinavian Airlines
International airline, Sweden. Designed by Stockholm Design Lab, 1998

34/ 35/ 36/

37/

33/Deutsche Bank
Financial services provider, Germany
Designed by Stankowski & Duschek, 1974
A corporate symbol for a bank, and subsequently for Western capitalism, the Deutsche Bank logo is the most widely exported creation of Anton Stankowski, a designer whose influence on the image of German industry is unrivalled. In the 1920s and 1930s, Stankowski was heavily influenced by constructivist art in his design, painting and photography. From the 1950s, he transferred the movement's principles of formal simplification and objectification of ideas and processes into what was then known as commercial art, designing numerous memorable logos for clients such as Viessmann, Deutsche Börse and SEL. The square held a special position in Constructivism, and Stankowski saw identity design as the perfect application of its visual properties: elemental simplicity, neutrality and symmetry. In 1972, he was one of eight designers asked to create a new logo for Deutsche Bank. His 'slash in a square', standing for consistent growth in a secure environment, was striking, fad-free and clearly recognizable at any size. In an old-fashioned industry that was having to transform itself fast, the mark positioned Deutsche Bank ahead of the game.

34/Expo Nova
Contemporary furniture retailer, Norway.
Designed by Mission Design, 2003

35/Space Genie
Flexible furniture system by MFI, UK. Designed by Bibliotheque, 2006

36/General Motors
Vehicle manufacturing group, USA. Designer unknown
GM's traditional blue badge was updated to this high-gloss 3D version in line with similar treatments of other carmakers' logos. Vehicles from all of GM's brands are now identified by this logo.

37/Zeiss
Optical systems manufacturer, Germany.
Designed by Carl Zeiss AG Corporate Communications, 1993
The missing lens-shaped segment is a subtle reminder of the company's line of business.

01/

02/

03/

04/

05/

06/

07/

08/

09/

10/

11/

12/

13/

01/Makita
Power tool
manufacturer, Japan.
Designed by Makita, 1991

02/NHS
National Health Service,
UK. Designed by
Moon Communications
(D: Richard Moon), 1990
One of the most
politically sensitive
design assignments.
Moon took a gamble
and proposed an almost
anonymous identity for
three reasons: ease of
application; durability;
and invisibility from
the British media,
to whom identity
programmes represent
an extravagant use
of public funds. The
NHS was persuaded,
and has saved 'tens of
millions of pounds'.

03/Skadden
Legal services group,
USA. Designed by
OH&Co, 2002
A snappier word mark
than the group's full
name: Skadden, Arps,
Slate, Meagher & Flom
LLP & Affiliates.

04/Duracell
Alkaline battery
manufacturer, USA.
Designed by Lippincott
Mercer, 1964

05/Western Digital
Hard drive
manufacturer, USA.
Designed 2004

06/USB CELL
Rechargeable AA
battery brand, UK.
Designed by
Turner Duckworth
(CD: David Turner, Bruce
Duckworth; D: Jamie
McCathie; typography:
Jeremy Tankard), 2005

07/Bern Billett
Ticket agency for
cultural events in Bern,
Switzerland. Designed
by Atelier Bundi, 2004

08/DevineCustom
Interior decorating
colour consultation
service, USA. Designed
by Sandstrom Design,
2006

09/Apotek
National association of
pharmacies, Denmark.
Designed by
Kontrapunkt, 2005

10/Die Pinakotheken
Art galleries, Germany.
Designed by KMS Team
(CD: Michael Keller;
D: Marion Fink), 2001
A system for three
related institutions:
a solid rectangle
for classical art (Die
Alte Pinakothek); an
emerging frame for the
increasing self-reflection
of 19th-century art
(Die Neue Pinakothek);
and four equal areas
for the pluralism of
contemporary art
(Die Pinakothek Der
Moderne).

**11/Ontario College of Art
& Design**
Art school, Toronto,
Canada. Designed by
Hambly & Woolley (CD:
Bob Hambly; DD: Barb
Woolley; D: Emese
Ungar-Walker), 2003
Architect Will Alsop's
'tabletop' building
addition is reflected in
the slab-like logo.

12/Deutsche Bahn
National railway,
Germany. Designed by
Kurt Weidemann, 1993
Weidemann designed
a 'stationary' logo,
deliberately unlike the
more dynamic emblems
of other railways,
as he felt the trains
themselves conveyed
the sense of speed. In
Germany, perhaps.

13/Slate
Credit card, UK.
Designed by Rose, 2005
The identity for a credit
card from retailer MFI
was inspired by a British
expression: debts are
'put on the slate', with
the hope of 'wiping
it clean' sometime in
the future.

01/

02/

03/

04/

05/

01/JS3D
Cinematic 3D and video effects for websites, UK. Designed by Sam Dallyn, 2006

02/Lightflow
E-commerce consultancy, USA. Designed by Segura Inc, 2003

03/Mitsubishi Motors
Carmaker, Japan. Designed by Yataro Iwasaki, 1870
Car-making under the Mitsubishi name goes back to 1917, but the company was founded as a shipbuilder by Yataro Iwasaki in 1870. 'Mitsu' means 'three' and 'hishi' means 'water chestnut', the traditional Japanese symbol for a diamond shape.

Together, they are spoken as 'mitsubishi'. Iwasaki chose the emblem for its similarity to both the three-leaf crest of the Tosa Clan, his first employer, and the three stacked rhombuses of his family crest. Today, the symbol is used by most of the companies in the Mitsubishi 'community'.

04/Georgia-Pacific
Pulp, paper and building products manufacturer, USA. Designer unknown

05/Tetra Pak
Food packaging systems, Switzerland. Designed by Toni Manhart and Jörgen Haglind, 1992
In 1992, Tetra Pak merged with Alfa Laval to create the Tetra Laval Group, whose mark is also a merger. Seen here with the Tetra Pak logotype, it combines an alpha symbol with a triangle.

06/Gepe
Photographic accessories company, Switzerland. Designed by Göran Pettersson, Per Lindström, 1955
Gepe's name was derived from the initials of the founder, Göran Pettersson. The original version of the logo featured two overlapping arrows, symbolizing the movement of the company's main product, a slide changer. In 1969, the arrowheads were removed, leaving two conjoined tails.

07/BKK
National association of company health insurance schemes, Germany. Designed by Stankowski & Duschek, 1988

08/Chase
Consumer and commercial banking services, USA. Designed by Chermayeff & Geismar Inc., 1961; proprietary typography and symbol revision by Sandstrom Design, 2006
Introduced in 1961, when few American corporations were identified by abstract symbols, the Chase octagon has survived a series of mergers.

09/Renault
Vehicle manufacturer, France. Designed by Éric de Berranger, 2004
The latest update of the rhomboid Renault logo, originally designed by Victor Vasarely to accompany the brand's relaunch with the Renault 5 in 1972, centres on a more lifelike 3D rendering of the badge.

10/

11/   12/   13/

index ◆

14/

10/DanceInTheCity.com
Website promoting
dance in Glasgow, UK.
Designed by Graphical
House, 2006

11/NYCE
Electronic payments
network, USA. Designed
by Siegel & Gale, 1984

12/Gulf Art Fair
Annual international
art fair, United Arab
Emirates. Designed by
Together Design (D:
Katja Thielen, Heidi
Lightfoot, Matt Savidge),
2006
Ancient Moorish
motifs are combined
with contemporary
typography.

13/DSM
Chemicals, materials
and nutritional products
manufacturer, The
Netherlands. Designer
unknown

14/Index
Mobile and media
services, Japan.
Designed by C&G
Partners (D: Emanuela
Frigerio), 2005

15/Kyocera
Electronic and ceramics
products manufacturer,
Japan. Designed by
Mitsuo Hosokawa, 1982
Introduced when Kyoto
Ceramic changed
its name to Kyocera,
the mark depicts a 'K'
wrapped around a 'C'.
The company adds,
colourfully: 'In various
cultures it has been said
to stand for each of the
following: the heart's
innermost region; a
starting point; Mother
Earth; the essence;
respect and dignity;
and a decision (as in
a flow chart).'

16/Christian Aid
International aid and
development charity,
UK. Designed by
Johnson Banks, 2006
Strangers to Christian
Aid wrongly perceived
it to be an evangelical
organization. The new
identity downplays the
word 'christian' and
makes a plea for aid, all
on a shape based on
the charity's most potent
symbol, the Christian Aid
Week envelope.

17/

18/

19/

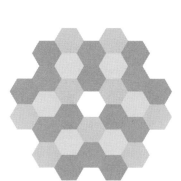

17/Central de Abasto
Wholesale market,
Mexico. Designed by
Lance Wyman, 1981
The identity and signage
system help legions
of visitors negotiate
the warehouses of
the world's largest
wholesale market.

18/Agfa
Imaging systems,
Belgium. Designed by
Agfa, 1923; revised by
Schlagheck & Schultes,
1984

19/Djøf
Trade union, Denmark.
Designed by Bysted,
2003
Danmarks Jurist- og
Økonomforbund is the
Danish Association
of Lawyers and
Economists.

20/D&AD
Educational charity, UK.
Designed by Rose, 2006
(original monogram:
Alan Fletcher, 1963)
A not-for-profit
organization, D&AD
invests in education and
award programmes to
promote good design
and advertising. The
updated logo positions
Alan Fletcher's
monogram within a
yellow hexagon, like
graphite in a yellow
pencil (D&AD's most
sought-after award).

21/Land Registry
British Government
database of property
ownership, UK. Designed
by North Design, 2003
The enormous task of
electronically recording
ownership of property
across England and
Wales was completed
in 2002. Today, the Land
Registry underpins the
British economy by
guaranteeing ownership
of property worth
billions of pounds. Its
database employs a
mapping system pattern
that plots the whole of
England and Wales in
interlocking hexagons.

01/

02/

03/

the global travel company

04/

05/

06/

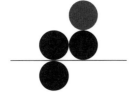

07/

08/

09/

10/ 11/ 12/

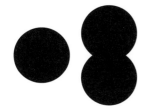  

13/ 14/ 15/

01/Nano-Tex
Textile manufacturer, USA. Designed by Addis Creson, 2003

02/Disaster Resource Network
Global humanitarian aid initiative, Switzerland. Designed by OH&Co, 2003
Launched by the World Economic Forum, the DRN channels donations from businesses to aid communities affected by natural disasters.

03/Zopa
Lending and borrowing exchange, UK. Designed by North Design, 2005
Rather like an Ebay for money, Zopa allows individuals to borrow money privately from the lender that offers the best interest rate. 'Zone of possible agreement' (Zopa) is an established term in sales and negotiation circles.

04/Radius
International travel agency, UK. Designed by Glazer, 2000

05/Metropolitan Transit Authority
Regional transport authority, USA. Designed by Siegel & Gale, 1993

06/Martha Stewart
Publishing, broadcasting and retailing group, USA. Designed by Doyle Partners, 2006
Inspired by antique coins, the logo suggests a small community around a table.

07/GJ Haerer
Fine printing and lithography service, USA. Designed by Chermayeff & Geismar Inc. (D: Emanuela Frigerio), 2001

08/Deutscher Ring
Insurance group, Germany. Designed by Stankowski & Duschek, 1969

09/Bob
Mobile phone service, Austria. Designed by Büro X (AD: Andreas Miedaner; D: Werner Singer), 2006
Referring to quality and price, 'Bob' stands for 'best of both'. An unusually human and minimal identity makes the brand easy to remember in a crowded marketplace.

10/Bosch
Industrial and consumer products group, Germany. Designed by Bosch, 1926; modified by United Designers, 2004
Based on the 'Bosch Service Lantern', the mark was first introduced in 1926 to signpost the company's car repair centres. United Designers freshened up the logo, thereby providing the basis for an overhaul of Bosch's communications.

11/Digital Lifestyle Outfitters
Computer and MP3 player accessories company, USA. Designed by DLO (D: Andrew Green) and Cabedge.com (D: Chris Blanz), 2004

12/Merck
Pharmaceutical group, USA. Designed by Chermayeff & Geismar Inc. (D: Audrey Krauss, Steff Geissbuhler), 1991

13/Antoine Brumel
Fashion retailer, Japan. Designed by Marvin (CD: Joan McCulloch; AD: Hiroki Yamamoto), 2006
An abstract 'a' and 'B'.

14/DO Nanbudo
Martial arts organization, Slovenia. Designed by OS Design Studio (D: Katarina Hribar), 2002
'D' represents the moon, the 'O' signifies the earth and the circle stands for the universe: the three interdependent cosmic elements at the heart of Nanbudo.

15/Ergosoft
Word-processing software developer, Japan. Designed by Marvin (CD: Joan McCulloch; AD: Hiroki Yamamoto), 2006

2.4 Circles and
dots

16/

17/

18/

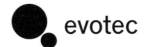

19/

20/

21/

London
Underground

22/

16/Océ
Printing systems, The
Netherlands. Designed
by Total Design (D: Wim
Crouwel), 1968; modified
by Baer Cornet, 1982

17/ABC
Television and radio
broadcasting group,
USA. Designed by Paul
Rand, 1962
Simple, direct and as
modern as a mark for
a TV network should
be, Rand's logo for the
American Broadcasting
Company picks up on
the natural visual rhythm
of the lower-case gothic
letterforms, underlined
by the equal circles
within each one.

18/General Electric
Technology and services
conglomerate, USA.
Designed by General
Electric Company, 1890s;
modified by Wolff Olins,
2004
Suggesting a new
format for corporate
signatures of an
acronym set within a
simple shape, this art
nouveau logo was
ahead of its time. It is
hard to imagine the GE
mark ever changing.

19/EA
Interactive
entertainment software
company, USA.
Designed by Michael
Osborne Design, 1999
The company-wide
logo is derived from
the earlier mark for
sub-brand EA Sports.

20/Evotec OAI
Drug discovery and
development company,
Germany. Designed by
KMS Team (CD: Knut
Maierhofer; D: Mark
Fernandes), 1999
An identity for the
merger between Evotec
BioSystems AG and
Oxford Asymmetry
International.

21/YOI
Sushi ingredient
supplier, Australia.
Designed by NB: Studio
(AD: Nick Finney, Ben
Stott, Alan Dye), 1998

22/London Underground
Underground railway
system, UK. Designed by
Edward Johnston, 1918
Visionary London
Underground boss Frank
Pick first commissioned a
typeface from Johnston
for use on directional
and information signs.
Johnston went on to
use the typeface to
define the proportions
of the roundel. The logo
became the sign for
every tube station and,
later, for every London
bus stop.

23/

24/

25/

26/

27/

MasterCard
Worldwide

4THERECORD

Sensata
Technologies

28/

29/

30/

31/

23/Barbican
Arts venue, UK.
Designed by North
Design (original concept
by Citigate Lloyd
Northover), 2001

24/Nissan
Carmaker, Japan.
Designed by
FutureBrand, 2000
A gleaming metallic
roundel that has been
part of the hugely
successful 'Nissan
Revival Plan' under
CEO Carlos Ghosn.

25/Innovation Norway
National innovation
promotion agency,
Norway. Designed by
Mission Design, 2004

26/Palm
Mobile computing
products, USA. Designed
by Turner Duckworth
(AD: David Turner, Bruce
Duckworth), 2005

**27/The Channel 4 British
Documentary Film
Foundation**
Fund supporting new
documentary film-
makers, UK. Designed
by Spin, 2004

**28/MasterCard
Worldwide**
Payment card services,
USA. Designed by
FutureBrand (CD:
Wally Krantz; DD:
Michelle Matthews;
D: Chris Slarkiewicz,
Steve Kim), 2006
MasterCard's globally
recognized emblem of
two interlocking circles
is joined by a third:
'a forward-moving
lens', 'illuminating
the breadth, depth
and forward-thinking
viewpoint of MasterCard
Worldwide'. (Reprinted
with permission of
MasterCard. All rights
reserved.)

29/4 The Record
Charity promoting
black role models, UK.
Designed by Airside,
2006

**30/Sensata
Technologies**
Sensing and protection
systems, USA. Designed
by Landor, 2006
When Texas Instruments
spun off its Sensors
& Controls Division,
the new independent
business took the
name Sensata, Latin
for 'those things gifted
with a sense'. The logo
includes the name in
Braille, the language
based on touch.

31/Joyco
Confectionery group,
Spain. Designed by
Pentagram (D: John
McConnell), 1999
With most of its business
outside Spain, General
de Confiteria took the
step of changing its
name to one more
suited to travel: Joyco.
The logo splits the name
in two and uses the
letters in a pair of circles
to suggest happy faces.

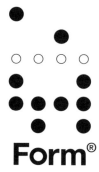

32/

33/

34/

35/

36/

32/Form
Graphic design
consultancy, UK.
Designed by Form (AD:
Paula Benson, Paul
West; D: Paul West), 2000

**33/MuseumsQuartier
Wien**
Umbrella organization
for Viennese cultural
venues, Austria.
Designed by Büro X (AD:
Andrea Miedaner; D:
Sascha Schaberl), 2000

34/New Audiences
Arts Council fund, UK.
Designed by Atelier
Works, 2000
A programme to support
the performance of
existing art, dance
and other productions
to new audiences in
shopping centres and
schools.

35/Fiat
Carmaker, Italy.
Designed by Robilant
Associati and the Fiat
Style Centre, 2006
Recalling the shield that
decorated Fiats from
1931 to 1968, the revised
logo has been made 3D.

36/Audi
Carmaker, Germany.
Designed 1932; updated
by MetaDesign, 1994
The four rings symbolize
the 1932 merger of four
independent carmakers:
Audi, DKW, Horch and
Wanderer.

37/SCP
Contemporary furniture
retailer, UK. Designed by
Peter Saville Associates,
1986

**38/Institute of
Contemporary Arts**
Art gallery and
performance venue, UK.
Designed by Spin, 2006
A bubbling-up of fresh
ideas in the arts and
a variety of activities
are alluded to in this
molecular-looking logo.

2.4 Circles and
dots

40/

41/

42/

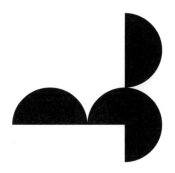

43/

39/Volkswagen
Carmaker, Germany
Designed by Franz Xaver Reimspiess, 1938;
modified by MetaDesign, 1996, 2000
The original authorship of the VW logo has long
been a bone of contention, since neither it nor
its creator has ever been registered officially.
However, following the dismissal of a claim for
recognition of copyright from Nikolai Borg that
came to court in Vienna in 2005, credit now rests
with Reimspiess, one of the carmaker's leading
engineers. Borg was a 20-year-old design student
in 1939 when, he claimed, the Nazi transport
minister, Fritz Todt, commissioned him to produce
a logo for the carmaker. The court heard, though,
that a design by Reimspiess had already been
submitted in a trademark application the previous
year, and was seen on hubcaps at the Berlin Auto
Show in April 1939. In early versions, the logo was
surrounded by the gear-shaped emblem of the
German Labour Front. The latest refinements by
MetaDesign include the logo's 3D highlights.

40/Theatre Brava!
Multi-purpose theatre,
Japan. Designed
by Shinnoske (AD:
Shinnoske Sugisaki;
CD: Mikio Uno; D: Chiaki
Okuno), 2005
Cheers and applause
are visualized in the
letters of Brava!

41/Bob Schalkwijk
Photographer, Mexico.
Designed by Wyman
& Cannan (D: Lance
Wyman), 1976

42/Smeg
Domestic appliance
manufacturer, Italy.
Designer unknown
Smeg is an acronym for
Smalterie Metallurgiche
Emiliane Guastalla:
meaning the metal-
enamelling plant of
Guastalla, Reggio
Emilia.

43/Moving Brands
Branding for various
media, UK. Designed by
Bibliotheque, 2004
A geometric abstraction
of the letters 'M' and 'B',
the logo has a circular
theme derived from
the shape of recording
media – spools, CDs
and DVDs.

01/

02/

03/

Learning & Performance

04/

05/

06/

07/

01/S&T
Software developer, Japan. Designed by Taste Inc (D: Toshiyasu Nanbu), 2000

02/GlaxoSmithKline
Pharmaceuticals and healthcare products manufacturer, UK. Designed by FutureBrand (CD: Paul Barlow), 2001
The merger of two pharma giants, GlaxoWellcome and SmithKline Beecham, demanded a new identity to appeal to consumer and professional markets without threatening the group's existing successful product brands. The egg-like shape and lower-case lettermarks present

a company keen to express its sensitivity to people and their well-being. (© [2001] by GlaxoSmithKline. Reprinted with permission of GlaxoSmithKline. All rights reserved.)

03/Esso
Fuels and lubricating oils, USA. Designer unknown, 1923
Esso remains (with Mobil) one of the primary brands of ExxonMobil outside the USA. Its name is derived from the phonetic pronunciation of 'SO', which stood for Standard Oil, one part of which eventually renamed itself Exxon Corporation.

04/Learning & Performance
Training consultancy, Japan. Designed by Taste Inc (D: Toshiyasu Nanbu), 2005

05/Confetti.co.uk
Online wedding guide, UK. Designed by Coley Porter Bell (CD: Stephen Bell), 2001

06/DEPS
Data management systems, Japan. Designed by Taste Inc (D: Toshiyasu Nanbu), 1990

07/Qua Baths & Spa
Spa and treatment rooms, USA. Designed by Addis Creson, 2006
Opened at Caesars Palace Las Vegas in November 2006, Qua aspires to be 'reminiscent of the glorious baths of ancient Rome' and to offer a 'live-in-the-moment philosophy', hence the name ('qua' means 'here' in Latin). The hand-painted logo suggests a watery experience.

2.5 Ovals and
ovoids

08/

09/

10/

11/

12/

13/

14/

08/Pfizer
Pharmaceutical
company, USA.
Designed by Enterprise
IG, 1991
More than 20 years of
growth and acquisitions
since the last review of
its corporate identity
had left Pfizer's
communications and
image confused and
fragmented. A new
identity system, headed
by a more assertive
'neo-traditional' blue
Pfizer oval, helped
to unite all of the
company's operating
units. For millions of
people, the logo now
represents a small
miracle, so close is its
resemblance to the blue
Viagra pills that have
carried the company
name since 1998.

09/Atox
Nuclear power station
radiation management
and waste disposal
service, Japan.
Designed by Katsuichi
Ito Design Studio, 1993

10/Gold Top
Recording studio, UK.
Designed by Crescent
Lodge, 2004
The studio's location in
a converted dairy led to
its name, Gold Top. Up
until the 1970s, a gold
foil top on a milk bottle
in the UK denoted high-
quality full-cream milk.
Even for those recording
artists too young to
remember, the name
and logo still retain an
aspirational quality.

11/Aerus
Vacuum cleaner
manufacturer, USA.
Designed by Addis
Creson, 2001

12/Vipp
Waste bin manufacturer,
Denmark. Designed by
e-types, 2006
The design of Vipp's
pedal bins has hardly
changed since 1939,
when craftsman Holger
Nielsen made one for
his wife's hairdressing
salon in Randers. Soon
everyone in the town
wanted one, and today
they are bought all over
the world. In 2006, to
coincide with the launch
of new products, Vipp
modernized its logo and
acquired its own family
of fonts.

13/FmN
Music festival, Belgium.
Designed by Coast, 2004
The Festival Musical
de Namur is a classical
music event held
annually in the capital
of Belgium's French-
speaking region. Closely
related to that of the
Théâtre de Namur, the
logo is also an oval
containing an 'N', but
with the addition of a
classical 'F' and an 'm'.

14/Intel
Semiconductor
manufacturer,
USA. Designed by
FutureBrand, (CD: Paul
Gardner; D: Sylvia Chu,
Rebecca Cobb, Ana
Gonzalez, Isabella
Ossott), 2006
The first redesign
of the Intel logo
since the company's
foundation capitalized
on the visibility of the
successful Intel Inside
brand. It appropriated
the 'swoosh', but turned
it into a full oval to
symbolize the cyclical
nature and the constant
improvement process of
research-development-
application.

2.6 Radiating

01/

02/

03/

04/

05/

06/

07/

01/Omega
Planned business park, UK. Designed by Coley Porter Bell (CD: Stephen Bell; D: Andrew Paterson), 2003 Omega is a planned £1-billion business community being developed over the next 25 to 30 years.

02/Global Cool
Climate change campaign, UK. Designed by SEA, 2006 Established by environmental entrepreneurs and scientists, the foundation aims to encourage a billion people to reduce their CO_2 emissions by one tonne by 2017, thereby postponing the tipping point of climate change.

03/StreetShine
Social enterprise for the homeless, UK. Designed by Coley Porter Bell (CD: Stephen Bell; D: Matt Gilpin), 2005 Homeless people are employed by StreetShine to operate a shoe-care and dry-cleaning service in offices and hotels across London. The maximalist logo incorporates the tools of the trade.

04/Sydney Youth Orchestra
Youth orchestra, Australia. Designed by Saatchi Design, 2006 A bundle of musical energy.

05/VSO
International development charity, UK. Designed by Spencer du Bois, 1993 VSO works in all parts of the world, hence the compass/sun element of the logo.

06/Motorola DigitalDNA
'Smart' product microchip systems, USA. Designed by Pentagram (D: Michael Bierut), 1998

07/Shell
Oil and gas production, The Netherlands. Designed by Raymond Loewy, 1971 'Shell' was originally the brand name for kerosene being shipped to the Far East by Marcus Samuel & Co of London. This small

business, based in the East End, had previously traded as a shop, dealing in exotic curios and oriental seashells, which became the basis for a successful import and export business with the Far East. In 1897, the company assumed the name 'Shell'. Its first logo was an uninspiring, flat mussel shell, but this was replaced by a scallop shell, or pecten, in 1904. Then, when 'Shell' Transport and Trading merged with the Royal Dutch Petroleum Company ten years later, it became the short form and visible emblem of the new Royal Dutch/Shell Group. In 1948, the word 'SHELL' was

emblazoned across the redrawn yellow pecten, which stood on a red background. Further refinements followed, until Raymond Loewy was approached in 1967 to make the logo more visible from a distance since cars were getting faster. Loewy streamlined the shell and placed the name below the pecten. So recognizable has Loewy's symbol become, that the name was dropped altogether in 1999.

Protestantse Kerk

Wild Circle

SAN FRANCISCO
OPERA

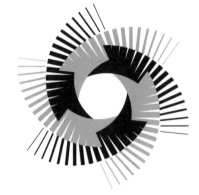

HUAWEI

SNOWSPORTGB

GRACE CATHEDRAL

bennett schneider
specialty greetings & paper

15/   16/   17/

18/

08/Protestantse Kerk
Dutch Protestant
Church, The
Netherlands. Designed
by Total Identity (D: Aad
van Dommelen), 2003

09/Wild Circle
TV production company,
UK. Designed by Form
(AD, D: Paula Benson;
D: Tom Hutchings), 2006

10/San Francisco Opera
Opera house and
company, USA.
Designed by Pentagram
(AD: Brian Jacobs;
D: Rob Duncan), 2005
A spectacular
chandelier in the opera
house lobby inspired
this burst of musical
light.

11/Shell Electric Storm
Wind-power installation,
UK. Designed by
Bibliotheque, 2004
An identity inspired by
a wind turbine was used
for an installation on
London's South Bank,
sponsored by Shell.

12/Huawei Technologies
Telecoms networks
producer, China.
Designed by Interbrand,
2006
The launch of this logo
threw the company – or
its consultants – into
semiotics overdrive.
A giant of China's
emerging economy,
Huawei explained
that 'the radiating
shapes...indicate
Huawei's commitment
to creating long-term
value for our customers',

and that by 'adopting
a graduated tone while
keeping symmetrical,
the new logo...acts
as a metaphor for
Huawei's open-minded
attitude and partnership
strategy'.

13/Heather Sayer
Manicurist and
pedicurist, UK. Designed
by Mind Design, 2005
The 'nail flower' for this
nail artist is inspired
by charts of nail polish
colours.

14/Snowsport GB
British Ski and
Snowboard Federation,
UK. Designed by Form
(CD: Matt Ryan, John
Rudaizky [Rudaizky
Ryan]; AD, D: Paul West;
D: Nick Hard), 2004

15/Grace Cathedral
Episcopal church, USA.
Designed by Templin
Brink Design (CD: Joel
Templin, Gaby Brink;
D: Ty Mattson), 2006
Celebrating its
centenary in 2007, this
San Francisco landmark
needed a welcoming
identity that conveyed
openness and a
searching spirit.

16/Sokol Blosser Winery
Winemaker, USA.
Designed by Sandstrom
Design, 1995

17/Bennett Schneider
Greetings card and
paper retailer, USA.
Designed by Design
Ranch (AD: Michelle
Sonderegger, Ingred
Sidie; D: Rachel Karaca),
2006
Designed to reflect the
beauty of fine paper.

18/London Innovation
Innovation promotion
agency, UK. Designed
by Kent Lyons, 2005

20/

21/

22/

23/

24/

25/

19/BP
Oil and gas production, UK
Designed by Landor Associates, 1999
There had to be a clean break from the BP of the past when the company 'merged' with Amoco in 1998. BP would no longer be short for 'British Petroleum'; the combined business was global in scale, among the world's largest private-sector energy companies. The traditional green and yellow shield was dropped. In various forms, it had served the business since 1920 when the then Anglo-Persian Oil Company marketed cans of motor fuel as BP, and a member of the purchasing department had won a staff competition to design a brand mark. In 1954, the company changed its name to BP, exploiting the visibility of the brand in advertising and on petrol pumps. The green colour scheme was brought in to better blend in with the British countryside; previously, pumps and trucks had been painted red. It was a fortuitous move: green would prove to be the colour to own for energy companies. In 1999, the new design was unveiled, with the letters 'bp' very much taking a back seat. The shape is variously claimed to be based on an image of the sun, a sunflower and a floor tile pattern at Britannic House (BP's former headquarters).

20/Spire Corporation
Diversified technology manufacturer, USA. Designer unknown
Spire produces solar-energy manufacturing equipment, medical devices and semi-conductors, all based on a common technology platform.

21/Galeria Fotonauta
International photography gallery, Spain. Designed by Lance Wyman, 2004
A camera lens composed of rectangular frames includes a north point to suggest a nautical compass.

22/Lifespan
Rhode Island hospitals alliance, USA. Designed by Malcolm Grear Designers, 1995

23/Christmas at W
Hotel's Christmas promotion, Australia. Designed by Layfield, 2006
Christmas is spent on the beach at the W Hotel Sydney.

24/Mexican Institute of Foreign Trade (IMCE)
Government ministry of exports, Mexico. Designed by Lance Wyman, 1971

25/VCC Perfect Pictures
Post-production company, Germany. Designed by Thomas Manss & Company, 1999
Alluding to the perception-altering abilities of post-production, this identity plays on a 19th-century optical illusion.

01/

02/

03/

04/

05/

06/

07/

01/Anglo American
International mining group, UK/South Africa. Designed by The Partners (AD: James Beveridge; D: Annabel Clements, Esther Rushton, David Richards, Ian Lankibury), 1999
To unify a diverse group of operating companies in several countries, Anglo American's new brand strategy focused on the company's core businesses: diamonds, gold, platinum and other natural resources. The logo represents not just the extraction of precious minerals but the group itself: multifaceted with high value at its core.

02/Coil
Electronica band, Japan. Designed by Form (AD: Paul West; D: Paul West, Nick Hard), 2003

03/CommonHealth
Healthcare marketing communications group, USA. Designed by Enterprise IG (DD: Dennis Thomas; SD: Atoussa Ghanbarzadeh), 2005
Designed to represent a network of focused, integrated operating units.

04/Ecological Engineering
Water resource management consultancy, Australia. Designed by Inkahoots, 2000

05/Novo Diem
Family organizational products, USA. Designed by Design Ranch (AD: Michelle Sonderegger, Ingred Sidie; D: Brynn Johnson), 2006

06/The ARChive of Contemporary Music
Not-for-profit music archive and library, USA. Designed by Open, 1996
The ARChive in Manhattan holds 1.5 million recordings from 1950 to the current day, making it the largest such collection in the USA. Its board of advisors includes David Bowie, Lou Reed, Paul Simon, Martin Scorsese and Keith Richards. When animated, the concentric arcs line up to present sound waves in two directions.

07/Conrail
Railway freight transporter, USA. Designed by Siegel & Gale, 1975
By the early 1970s, freight services in the north-east USA had gone bankrupt or were nearing the end of the line. The government agreed to provide interim funding to help get the services running profitably again as the new Consolidated Rail Corporation, or Conrail. The visual identity is classic American modernism: economic but emphatic. It conveyed the idea of an enterprise that was back on track and moving smoothly at speed. By the 1980s, the company was in the black, and,

in 1987, the largest initial public offering in American history saw Conrail's stock sold to private investors.

⦿ CloudShield™

08/

09/

10/

JFE

**NetzwerkHolz
Qualität
im Verbund**

08/CloudShield Technologies
Network protection and security systems, USA. Designed by Pentagram (CD: Kit Hinrichs; D: Erik Schmitt), 2001

09/Hear US
National campaign for hearing health, USA. Designed by Chermayeff & Geismar Inc. (D: Steff Geissbuhler), 2000

10/Seagate Technologies
Computer hard drive manufacturer, USA. Designed by Landor Associates, 2002 Suggestions of disks, data and high-speed rotation appear in this logo, which signalled Seagate's new integrated manufacturing strategy.

11/Cass Business School
Business school, UK. Designed by Crescent Lodge, 2002 Five rings denote separate areas of activity within the Cass Business School. The rings sit in relationship to each other according to a mathematical sequence based on the Fibonacci numbers, generating the image of the City of London as an 'intellectual hub'.

12/JFE Group
Steel producer, Japan. Designed by Bravis International, 2002

13/Overture
Internet search engine, USA. Designed by Chermayeff & Geismar Inc. (D: Emanuela Frigerio, Frank Dylla), 2002

14/NetzwerkHolz
National wood industry association, Germany. Designed by KMS Team (CD: Knut Maierhofer; D: Mark Fernandes), 2004 Tree rings suggest growth and influence for NetzwerkHolz, Germany's frst general association of lumber producers, woodworkers and craftsmen.

01/

02/   03/   04/

05/

noriksub

07/

08/

09/

01/Professional Energy
Oil trading consultancy, USA. Designed by Design Ranch (AD: Michelle Sonderegger, Ingred Sidie; D: Rachel Karaca), 2006

02/Charles B Wang Asian American Center
Multiculturalism centre at the State University of New York at Stony Brook, USA. Designed by HLC Group (D: Hoi L Chu), 1997

03/e&a Optical Disc
CD, DVD and packaging printer, USA. Designed by Malone Design (D: David Malone), 2006

04/Delta Faucet
Tap manufacturer, USA. Designed by Pentagram (D: Woody Pirtle), 2001

05/Transammonia
Marketer and shipper of fertilisers, ammonia and petrochemicals, USA. Designed by Arnold Saks Associates, 1969

06/Norik Sub
Diving school and scuba shop, Slovenia. Designed by OS Design Studio (D: Toni Kancilja, Katarina Hribar), 2004 Waves or tentacles? The delights of the deep in a single symbol.

07/Mizarstvo Rozman
Furniture workshop, Slovenia. Designed by OS Design Studio (D: Katarina Hribar), 1998

08/The Corner Store
Online software retailer, USA. Designed by HLC Group (D: Hoi L Chu), 1995
A 'C' and an 'S' in a pinwheel, the logo is cut out for visibility in hot links and on the desktop.

09/Palm Beach Couture
Fashion swimwear retailer, Australia. Designed by Layfield Design
This label's swimwear reflects the glamour of Sydney's exclusive Palm Beach. The logo, an abstraction of a palm leaf and ocean waves, attempts to match the iconic quality of the marks for such luxury brands as Chanel and Louis Vuitton.

2.9 Dotted patterns

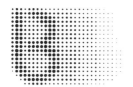

02/

03/

04/

05/

06/

07/

01/Seed Media Group
Scientific publisher, USA
Designed by Sagmeister Inc (CD: Stefan Sagmeister;
AD, D: Matthias Ernstberger), 2005
Stefan Sagmeister is best known in the design world
for the visceral, handmade, almost primitive images
that his studio produced in the 1990s. This is the
man who, when designing a poster to advertise
a lecture he was giving, asked an assistant to
inscribe the details onto his (Sagmeister's) naked
torso with a scalpel and then photograph their
handiwork. His work on CD covers for David Byrne
and Lou Reed has also won awards. Recently,
though, he has turned his attention to identity
design and larger, more mainstream audiences.
In 2006, he told the online magazine 'designboom.
com', 'I would love to redesign the Coke can,
or an identity that is truly "worldwide"....Today,
how children learn what the world looks like is
determined by these type of jobs.' His identity
for Seed Media Group could prove a stepping
stone to bigger things. Based on phyllotaxis, the
arrangement of leaves on an axis or stem, the
logo encapsulates Seed's watchword: 'Science
is culture'.

02/Bedrock Records
Record company, UK.
Designed by Malone
Design (D: David
Malone), 2003
Picking up on the visual
output of graphic
equalizers, the logo
is for use on the
company's record and
CD sleeves.

**03/Partner für
Innovation**
Federal government
campaign, Germany.
Designed by
MetaDesign, 2005
'Innovative impulse'
is symbolized by this
mark for a German
government campaign
to stimulate new ideas
in business.

**04/University Science
Park Pebble Mill**
Science park
development, UK.
Designed by Brownjohn
(D: James Beveridge,
Andy Mosley), 2005
An identity for a science
park to be built on the
site of the former BBC
studios at Pebble Mill,
Birmingham.

05/Universität Stuttgart
Science- and
engineering-led
university, Germany.
Designed by Stankowski
& Duschek, 1987

06/Captive Resources
'Group captive'
insurance company
advisors, USA. Designed
by Crosby Associates,
2006

07/e-Parliament
Online forum for
legislators, Belgium.
Designed by Open, 2002
The e-Parliament is
designed to bridge
the 'democracy gap'
between citizens
and decision-making
at national and
international levels. It
is a Brussels-based
council, composed
of legislators from
countries around the
world who are selected
through an online
voting system.

2.10 Horizontal
stripes

01/

02/

03/

04/

05/

06/

07/

NIGHTLIFE.BE

08/

09/

10/

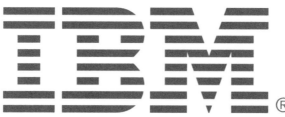

11/

01/Münchener Rück
Reinsurance group, Germany. Designed by Stankowski & Duschek, 1973
For the firm better known as Munich Re, Anton Stankowski created a logo of parallel bars that form a square to symbolize connection and exchange, partnership and interaction, work and enterprise.

02/Simon & Schuster Editions
Illustrated book publishing imprint, USA. Designed by Eric Baker Design Associates (CD, D: Eric Baker), 2001

03/Strassburger Modeaccessories
Fashion accessories label, Germany. Designed by Büro Uebele Visuelle Kommunikation, 2004
Stripes as tassels, letters as beads.

04/G&B Printers
Printer, UK. Designed by North Design, 2004
The overprinted company address was originally created during the use of a two-company stationery set. When one company used the stationery, the other's details were blocked out using different print materials and processes. Anonymity breeds individuality.

05/Ohio State University Knowlton School of Architecture
Architecture school, USA. Designed by Fitch (D: Garrick Reischman), 2004

06/EDB
IT group, Norway. Designed by Mission Design, 2003

07/Dictionary.com
Online English dictionary, USA. Designed by Segura Inc, 2005

08/Phatspace
Art gallery, Australia. Designed by Coast Design (Sydney), 2002
Like a gallery, the logo presents a space to be transformed. Flyers for exhibitions are treated as an opportunity to experiment rather than to reproduce artworks.

09/Nightlife.be
Website, Belgium. Designed by Coast, 2003
Paying homage to the IBM logotype, this mark is a nostalgic reinterpretation of the computer screen.

10/Lucy Lee Quality Recordings
Record label, Belgium. Designed by Coast, 2005
The company's music is diverse enough to evade easy labelling, a fact that is reflected in the logo where the words 'Lucy' and 'Lee' are blanked out. Applied on sleeves that all feature full-bleed photographs of parts of the body, the mark assumes a second life as a pair of sticking plasters.

11/IBM
Computing technology and services, USA. Designed by Paul Rand, 1962
IBM's timeless eight-stripe logotype was arrived at in stages. While designing print materials for the company in the mid-1950s, Rand lightened the existing slab-serif logo. Aware that sudden change would alienate the IBM board, Rand waited several years before venturing a striped version. Its connotations of security (anti-forgery measures on signed documents) and its quality of visually 'tying together' the heavy competing letterforms won the day.

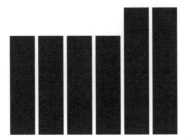

01/

02/

03/

GARTNER

newtown flicks

04/ 05/ 06/

Swiss Re

07/

01/The Mill
Post-production and visual effects company, UK. Designed by North Design, 1999
Letterforms from lengths of film.

02/Haunch of Venison
Art gallery, UK. Designed by Spin, 2003
Reduction goes a step further: a minimalist 'HV' and a deer with a haunch missing.

03/Lantern
Residential property development, UK. Designed by Bibliotheque, 2006
Reflected in the logo are the development's division into twin buildings and its distinctive rectangular-panelled cladding.

04/Gartner
Building cladding systems, Germany. Designed by Büro für Gestaltung Wangler & Abele and Eberhard Stauß, 1993
A single mark captures the repetitive nature of a building façade and of the industrial production of cladding panels.

05/Newtown Flicks
Short film festival, Australia. Designed by Saatchi Design, 2005

06/Donemus
National institution for composed contemporary music, The Netherlands. Designed by Samenwerkende Ontwerpers (D: André Toet), 2005

07/Swiss Re
Reinsurance firm, Switzerland. Designed by Büro für Gestaltung Wangler & Abele and Eberhard Stauß, 1994
A logo that is simple and unique but which the company itself is keen to stress has no symbolic significance. However, the suggestion of Stonehenge-like stability and impregnability is unmistakable.

2.11 Vertical stripes

a|s'te,rdo,r'f

a|titude

09/

10/

11/

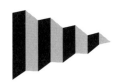

URBAN**SPACE**

12/

13/

14/

08/Mika Ohtsuki
Piano technician, USA
Designed by Emmi, 2005
Committees and large groups of marketing people are more likely to produce compromise than memorable strokes of creativity. Most of the classic logo designs were created by single, visionary minds or very small groups comprising the client's principal decision-maker(s) and a designer. In the case of this logo there were just two people involved: Mika Ohtsuki, a New York-based piano technician, and Emmi Salonen, a Finnish graphic designer based at the time in the USA. The final solution features five ebony piano keys, one of which is slightly out of place and in need of tuning. It also spells out the client's initials. 'Identity design,' says the designer, 'feels like a puzzle where I have to find the core of my client's business visually and then find a contrast to this. I end up with two elements to play with and I have to find a way to fit these together. Sometimes a project comes along where the existing visual language of associations is so strong, it's easy to keep the solution minimal. Saying that, it took me a while to come to this solution and I thought I had it with something else first. But I kept working on it – and I'm glad I did.'

09/Evangelische Stiftung Alsterdorf
Charitable foundation for disabled people, Germany. Designed by Büro Uebele Visuelle Kommunikation, 2006
Developed for a family of 60 organizations, this system of logos treats each member as a unique musical chord. The marks are created by registering the space between each pair of characters as a solid bar.

10/Altitude
Bespoke event and travel company, UK. Designed by Brownjohn (D: James Beveridge, Andy Mosley), 2006

11/I Need Help
Management consultancy, Ireland. Designed by The Stone Twins, 2005
A company's need for business assistance may not be immediately obvious, a fact reflected in this logo, where the space between the vertical bars spells out the consultancy's initials.

12/Arts Aimhigher in London
Higher education campaign, UK. Designed by Blast, 2005
Eight specialist arts institutions in London joined together to encourage groups of young people unaccustomed to higher education to reach new heights at art college.

13/Lienke
Recycling company, Germany. Designed by Thomas Manss & Company, 1986
A corrugated copper flag recalls Lienke's origins as a scrap-metal dealer in the late 19th century.

14/Urban Space
Real estate firm, USA. Designed by Lodge Design, 2006

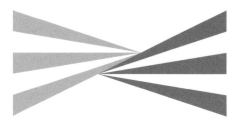

01/

SILVERSTONE

accutrack

02/   03/   04/

05/

 Promecon

M. J. T. P.

FAST RETAILING

06/   07/   08/

09/

01/Hager Group
Voltage distribution and electrical equipment company, Germany. Designed by Stankowski & Duschek, 1998

02/Silverstone
Motor racing circuit, UK. Designed by Carter Wong Tomlin, 2002
The dynamism and excitement of events at the home of British Grand Prix is captured in this mark.

03/Aviva
Insurance group, UK. Designed by Corporate Edge, 2001
Aviva was the name given to the business resulting from the merger of CGU and Norwich Union in 2000.

04/Accutrack
Rail track renewals service, UK. Designed by Roundel (D: Mike Denny, Richard Coward), 2004

05/Skirl Records
Artist-run experimental jazz record label, USA. Designed by karlssonwilker inc. (AD, D: Hjalti Karlsson, Jan Wilker), 2006

06/Promecon
Steel structure fabricator, Denmark. Designed by Bysted, 2001

07/Mizushima Joint Thermal Power
Thermal power generating company, Japan. Designed by Katsuichi Ito Design Studio, 1995

08/Fast Retailing
Clothing retailing group, Japan. Designed by Samurai (D: Kashiwa Sato), 2006
The logo for Japan's largest clothes retailer, best known for the Uniqlo brand.

09/Parc La Villette
Cultural park, France. Designed by Johnson Banks, 2000
A logo that functions as an edge for other visual communications, such as posters, web pages and banners. When it appears on the left, right or bottom edge, it offers new angles for text, images and other graphics.

01/

02/

03/

04/

05/

06/

07/

08/

09/

DUBAI
SPORTS
CITY

10/

11/

12/

HOYA

SEGA SAMMY
H O L D I N G S

13/

14/

15/

01/Sprint
Mobile communications, USA. Designed by Lippincott Mercer, 2006

02/Nike
Sports footwear and clothing manufacturer, USA. Designed by Carolyn Davidson, 1971; modified by Nike, 1978, 1985
The tale of how Nike got its 'swoosh' for $35 is part of design folklore. Nike founder Phil Knight bumped into Davidson in a corridor at Portland State University. She was working on a drawing assignment and Knight asked her to design a presentation about his fledgling sports-shoe business. Later, he asked for ideas

for a shoe stripe that suggested movement. None of her designs were right, he felt, but, up against a deadline and needing a logo for a batch of shoeboxes, he picked the 'swoosh'. 'I don't love it, but it will grow on me,' he told her. She submitted her modest bill for $35. In 1983, Knight presented Davidson with the gift of a gold 'swoosh' ring and an undisclosed quantity of Nike stock.

03/Bridge
Internal communications programme, UK. Designed by Rose, 2004
Belron International – the world's leading car glass company – undertook a global initiative to establish a standardized IT platform across all its businesses.

04/Enbridge
Energy distributor, Canada. Designed by Lippincott Mercer, 1998
A new name was needed to replace IPL Energy and to unify a decentralized organization. Enbridge is a fusion of 'energy' and 'bridge'.

05/Acela
Amtrak's high-speed rail service, USA. Designed by OH&Co, 1999

06/Thomas Telford
Civil engineering publisher, UK. Designed by Spencer du Bois (D: John Spencer), 2006

07/Rbk
Fashion-conscious sports footwear and clothing manufacturer, USA. Designed by Arnell Group, 2001

08/Skischule Alpendorf
Ski school, Austria. Designed by Modelhart Design, 2003

09/Besix
Construction group, Belgium. Designed by Total Identity (D: Léon Stolk), 2004

10/Shire
Speciality pharmaceuticals company, UK. Designer unknown

11/Dubai Sports City
Purpose-built sports city, United Arab Emirates. Designed by FutureBrand Melbourne and FutureBrand Dubai, 2005

12/J Power
Privatized electricity supplier, Japan. Designed by Bravis International, 2002

13/Hoya
Optics manufacturer, Japan. Designed by Bravis International, 2000

14/Miyazaki
Lumber producer, Japan. Designed by Kokokumaru, 1998

15/Sega Sammy Holdings
Computer games developer, Japan. Designed by Bravis International, 2004

01/

02/

03/

CREDIT SUISSE

VitalTouch

FEEL LIFE

BLACKSTONE
technology group

04/

05/

06/

amBX

07/

01/Inscape
Investment management
services, UK. Designed
by North Design, 1999
Inscape offers specialist
financial advice to
people with more than
£50,000 to invest. Its
symbol represents
three concepts:
independence,
individuality and
investment.

02/Web Liquid
Digital marketing
agency, UK. Designed
by Bibliotheque, 2004
Forming the 'Q' in the
company's wordmark,
the symbol was inspired
by a hydrogen molecule.

03/Nectar
Retail loyalty reward
scheme, UK. Designed
by Corporate Edge, 2001

04/Credit Suisse
Financial services,
Switzerland. Designed
by Enterprise IG, 2006
A single brand was
needed for the entire
group of banking
businesses in the Credit
Suisse Group. The
abstract sail device is
intended to recall the
former identity of Credit
Suisse First Boston,
'while conveying the
notion of pioneering
and navigation'.

05/Vital Touch
Organic aromatherapy
and massage products,
UK. Designed by Ico
Design, 2006

**06/Blackstone
Technology Group**
IT services consultancy,
USA. Designed by
Templin Brink Design
(CD: Joel Templin, Gaby
Brink; D: Paul Howalt),
1999

07/amBX
Ambient gaming system,
UK. Designed by
BB/Saunders, 2005
Developed by Philips,
amBX is a new
technology that uses
surround lighting,
sound, vibration, air
movement and other
effects to create an
'ambient experience'
for gamers. The identity
sought to express the
technology's latent
'intelligence' while
being robust enough
to potentially represent
a global industry
standard, in a similar
vein to the Dolby and
Compact Disc symbols.

2.14 Amorphous

08/

09/ 10/ 11/

12/

08/Dragoncloud
Organic tea collection, UK. Designed by Pentagram (D: David Hillman), 2001
A fragrant puff of steam rises from a cup of Dragoncloud artisan-made tea.

09/Cygnific
KLM Royal Dutch Airlines' customer-care arm, The Netherlands. Designed by Total Identity (D: Léon Stolk), 2001

10/Tatumi
Gas fuel supplier, Japan. Designed by Taste Inc (D: Toshiyasu Nanbu), 2004

11/Filippa K Ease
Fashion label, Sweden. Designed by Stockholm Design Lab, 2006
A restless soul: the identity for Filippa K's Ease label comprises still images of an animated digital flower, and is applied to bags and packaging.

12/Yauatcha
Chinese restaurant, UK. Designed by North Design, 2003
The identity for Alan Yau's upmarket Oriental eaterie was inspired by the undulating terraced terrain of the tea plantations of Long Jing in China. Equally, customers might see in it a cloud of dim-sum steam.

13/Dutch Infrastructure Fund
Investment fund for public-private partnership projects, The Netherlands. Designed by Studio Bau Winkel, 2004

14/Progreso
Fairtrade coffee bar chain, UK. Designed by Graven Images, 2004

15/h₂Hos
Feminist synchronized swimming team, USA. Designed by Marc English Design, 2004
Texas-based, the h₂Hos are a group of artists, activists, graduate students, mothers and social workers inspired by watching an Esther Williams' movie 'to re-present feminism through the aquatic arts'.

16/Spout
Online film community, USA. Designed by BBK Studio, 2005

Representational

The corporations represented in this section could hardly be called faceless. You will not find many subtle typographical twists or suggestive abstractions here. These are organizations that have been able to summarize in a single image what they stand for, what they do or the benefit they bring to customers.

Steff Geissbuhler, creator of NBC's rainbow-coloured peacock and the Time Warner eye/ear, is in no doubt about the advantages of an illustrative approach. He believes that 'actual symbols mean more today than abstractions. My NBC peacock still works today because people relate to something they can understand right away.' But that is not the whole story. A symbol that is easily understood can be successful without making any direct or obvious link to the entity it is representing. Apple's apple, MSN's butterfly and Starbucks' siren are three such enigmas.

Saul Bass was also of the view that a symbol should keep a little in reserve. He maintained that an element of visual ambiguity would keep viewers interested. The success of such symbols as Bass's for Minolta and the Adidas trefoil proves the value of being a little cryptic. If a logo is to be descriptive, it needs an X factor to be memorable. Tom Geismar, designer of symbols for Mobil Oil, Chase Manhattan Bank and Xerox, said that his aim with every logo is to design something that has 'some barb to it that will make it stick in your mind, make it different from the others'.

Many of the world's most idiosyncratic and best-known symbols have received their 'barb' from unexpected quarters. The logos of Coca-Cola, Bayer, WWF and Mercedes-Benz are all innocent scribbles that went nuclear and turned into global icons. And the equally iconic symbols for Amnesty International, NASA, UBS and Woolmark were by individuals who all made just one telling contribution to design history, and left.

AUSTRALIAN WILDLIFE
HOSPITAL

01/

02/

03/

04/

strc

filmaid
INTERNATIONAL

05/

06/

07/

patient choice
what's best for you

S✝ Kea

Universitätsklinikum
Erlangen

01/Australian Wildlife Hospital
Animal conservation, Australia. Designed by Coast Design (Sydney), 2005

02/Presbyterian Church (USA)
Church, USA. Designed by Malcolm Grear Designers, 1985
A remarkable fusion of symbols, each one relevant to the church: the Celtic cross, scripture, flames and a descending dove. Looking even closer, a fish and a baptismal font can also be made out.

03/SPR+ (Super Plus)
Fashion and lifestyle retailer, The Netherlands. Designed by smel, 2006

04/Alove
The Salvation Army's youth ministry, UK. Designed by Browns, 2004.
The Salvation Army is a church and registered charity in the UK that demonstrates its Christian principles through social welfare provision. Young people were found to be alienated by its traditional image of brass bands, bonnets and uniforms. Alove – pronounced with a soft 'a', as in 'alive' and 'above' – is the Army's

renamed youth ministry, conceived to encourage a better dialogue with a more youthful audience.

05/Scottish Track Renewals Company
Scottish rail infrastructure contractor, UK. Designed by Roundel (D: Mike Denny, Andy Hills), 2005
The allusion to the flag of St Andrew, through two rails crossing, signifies the Scottish arm of Jarvis Rail.

06/Filmaid International
Non-profit film screening organization, USA. Designed by Eric Baker Design Associates (CD, D: Eric Baker; D: Eric Strohl), 2005
Filmaid is a consortium of film-makers that brings education and entertainment, through film screenings, to traumatized communities and refugee camps in Africa.

07/Musée de Dragon
Fashion store, Japan. Designed by Kokokumaru (D: Yoshimaru Takahashi), 2005

08/Dez Mona
Vocal and double bass duo, Belgium. Designed by Emmi, 2005

09/Ski & Støveldoktoren
Ski and snowboard repair centre, Norway. Designed by Mission Design, 2006

10/Patient Choice
Government health initiative, UK. Designed by Purpose, 2005

11/St Kea
Church, UK. Designed by Arthur-SteenHorneAdamson (D: Marksteen Adamson, Scott McGufhe), 2004
In the logo for this Cornwall church, the cross stands in for a letter. On a range of branded goods and communications, it acts as a divine copyright symbol, claiming ownership for God's Kingdom of

profanities and over-used expressions such as 'bloody hell' and 'heavens above'.

12/University of Illinois Medical Center
University hospital, USA. Designed by Crosby Associates, 2001

13/Universitätsklinikum Erlangen
University hospital, Germany. Designed by Büro für Gestaltung Wangler & Abele, 2004

15/
·····

16/
·····

17/
·····

18/
·····

14/Bayer
Pharmaceutical and chemical company, Germany
Designed by Bayer, 1904; updated by Claus Koch
Corporate Communications, 2002
The Bayer Cross is one of those logos that is
unlikely ever to change, save for the occasional
minor tweak. Not even Bayer knows the original
author. Its archive names two possible designers:
Hans Schneider, working in the scientific
department in 1900, is documented as having
sketched it while in conversation one day; and
Dr Schweizer of the New York office, who wanted
an eye-catching emblem to aid his marketing
efforts, is also mentioned. Whichever account is
true, the symbol was registered in 1904 and, in 1910,
started to appear on Bayer's tablets as a sign of
quality and integrity. In 1929, the italic letters were
straightened, and, in 1933, the logo lit up the city of
Leverkusen when a Bayer cross, 72m in diameter
and boasting 2,200 light bulbs (the world's largest
illuminated sign), was hung between two chimney
stacks. Blackout regulations in 1939 signalled its
demise, but a new 51m-diameter cross was erected
in 1958 and still illuminates the skyline. The latest
update to the logo added colour – green and
blue – for the first time in its history and some
3D shading.

15/Alta Pampa
Importer of Latin
American art and crafts,
UK. Designed by Emmi,
2006
Crosses relate to the
patterns and textures
found in handwoven
Latin American fabrics
and contrast with the
contemporary lower-
case Western logotype.

16/Tazo
Tea company, USA.
Designed by Sandstrom
Design, 1994

**17/Creative Interventions
In Health**
Visual arts programme
for Glasgow healthcare
facilities, UK. Designed
by Graphical House,
2006

18/Milk
'Electro baroque' bar,
Belgium. Designed by
Coast, 2004

MORE TH>N

02/   03/   04/

05/

01/Nederlandse Spoorwegen
National rail network, The Netherlands
Designed by Tel Design (D: Gert Dumbar), 1968
Arrows are over-used devices in corporate
identity design. They are seen as something of a
positive-looking, fall-back option by organizations
whose activities are deemed too arcane for easy
encapsulation. For modernizing railways of the
1960s, however, they signalled dynamism, simplicity
and a progressive spirit, and yielded some of the
era's most potent and enduring corporate symbols.
The logo for the Dutch Railway followed hard on
the heels of Design Research Unit's 1965 British Rail
symbol, with its two-way arrow. Gert Dumbar's draft
designs included multiple combinations of the 'N'
and 'S' of Nederlandse Spoorwegen, but the image
of twin arrows neatly creating a closed system was
finally chosen. It seemed fitting for an organization
in the midst of reform to become more customer
friendly and market driven. The outcry from the
Dutch public, which had been used to a fuddy-
duddy rail company, was brief. In the UK, the old
BR logo is now only seen on traffic signs for railway
stations. In The Netherlands, the NS logo and yellow
and black colour scheme still drives a vibrant image
for train travel.

**02/Arts›World Financial
Center**
Visual and performing
arts venue, USA.
Designed by Open, 2006

03/Entry
Educational institution,
Brazil. Designed by
FutureBrand BC&H, 2006

04/More Th›n
Insurance company, UK.
Designed by Johnson
Banks, 2000
This company's hugely
(and unexpectedly)
successful launch
was due in part to the
logo's substitution of
a mathematical 'more
than' symbol in place of
an 'A', which makes for
an easily remembered
mark.

05/National Express
Scheduled coach
services, UK. Designed
by Dragon Brands, 2003

06/

07/

08/

09/

10/

11/

12/

13/

14/

Express

CITROËN

amazon.com.

06/Roam
Electronic road toll system, Australia. Designed by FutureBrand Melbourne, 2005

07/WCVB-TV Channel 5
TV station, USA. Designed by Wyman & Cannan (D: Lance Wyman), 1971

08/Gravity Flooring
Contract flooring company, UK. Designed by The Partners (AD: Nina Jenkins; D: Steve Owen, James Harvey, Leon Bahrani, Kate Shepherd), 2005

09/Heritage Information
Directory of historic building contractors, UK. Designed by Carter Wong Tomlin, 2002
An online database of companies approved to work on the renovation and reclamation of historic properties.

10/Chevron Corporation
Oil and gas group, USA. Designed by Lippincott Mercer, 1969; updated by Lippincott Mercer, 2005
In 1931, Standard Oil Company of California adopted a three-bar chevron logo in red white and blue. The chevron had positive associations, ranging from a motif in ancient art to the ranking system in the armed services.

The business became synonymous with the brand of its petrol stations and eventually changed name.

11/Kunsthal Rotterdam
Art gallery and museum, The Netherlands. Designed by Tel Design (D: Ronald van Lit), 1992

12/LogisticsNet Berlin Brandenburg
Public-private logistics network, Germany. Designed by Thomas Manss & Company, 2006
Boxes + motion = logistics.

13/SoCo
Property development, UK. Designed by 300Million (CD: Matt Baxter; D: Katie Morgan), 2006.
This mark was designed for a development that hoped to revive a district of central Edinburgh.

14/Burton Snowboards
Snowboard manufacturer, USA. Designed by Jager Di Paola Kemp, 2007
A fittingly acrobatic arrow.

15/Imagebank
Rights-managed photo library, UK. Designed by North Design, 2000

16/Dunlop Sport
Sports equipment manufacturer, UK. Designer unknown

17/Next
Internet consultancy, France. Designed by Area 17, 2003

18/FedEx
Courier service, USA. Designed by Landor Associates, 1994
According to designer Lindon Leader, one of the reasons that this logo was chosen over several others was because FedEx CEO Fred Smith was the only executive in a room of 12 to spot the arrow between the 'E' and 'x'. To create it, new letterforms and a new font had to be designed:

a combination of Univers 67 (Bold Condensed) and Futura Bold.

19/Citroën
Carmaker, France. Designed by André Citroën, 1919
Citroën's chevrons are descendents of the pointed teeth on the smooth-running 'herringbone' gears designed by founder André Citroën and used in the early vehicles.

20/Amazon.com
Online retailer, USA. Designed by Turner Duckworth, 2000
Everything, from A to Z, delivered with a smile.

22/
23/
24/

25/
26/
27/

21/Swiss Federal Railway
National rail network, Switzerland
Designed by Hans Hartmann, 1972; modified by
Uli Huber, 1976 and Josef Müller-Brockmann
and Peter Spalinger, 1978
Some graphic designers dream of being Swiss; not
necessarily for the skiing or fondue evenings, but
for the systematic, reductionist visual sensibility
that, when it emerged in the 1940s and 1950s, sent
shock waves through the design establishment.
The purity, intensity and discipline of posters and
publications designed by figures such as Armin
Hofmann, Josef Müller-Brockmann and Carlo
Vivarelli continues to influence new generations
of designers. A related reason for Swiss-envy is
the country's square flag, whose bold equilateral
white cross is a positive asset in branding national
institutions. The logo for SBB (Schweizerische
Bundesbahnen) brings the Swiss movement, Swiss
flag and the three Swiss languages together in a
model of democratic and quietly striking design.

22/NatWest.
Retail bank, UK.
Designed by HSAG,
1970; updated by
The Partners (AD: Gill
Thomas, Tony De Ste
Croix; D: Nina Jenkins,
Kate Hutchison, Tracy
Avison, Nick Eagleton,
Kevin Lan), 2003
When Royal Bank
of Scotland bought
NatWest in 2000, the
three-arrowhead
identity commanded
a remarkable 90%
recognition. It could
not be dropped, but
the bank was seen
as dull, faceless and
institutional. Colouring
the symbol red and
adding highlights
to the arrowheads
suggested that the bank
had developed some
personality and warmth.

23/Nike Shox
Retail campaign, UK.
Designed by Spin, 2002

24/ProSiebenSat.1
TV broadcasting group,
Germany. Designed by
KMS Team (CD: Knut
Maierhofer; D: Bruno
Marek)
A logo for the merger
of two networks
– ProSieben and
Sat.1 – combines the
numerals of both (7 and
1) into a single optimistic
arrow.

25/OCR Headway
Qualifications
assessment and
development
consultancy, UK.
Designed by Spencer
du Bois, 2004

**26/National Research
and Development Centre
for Adult Numeracy and
Literacy**
Educational
consultancy, UK.
Designed by Crescent
Lodge, 2002
Like FedEx, the NRDC
opted for a less obvious
kind of arrow. Whether
that feature is seen or
not, the emphatic logo
can be 'read' easily by
its audience, of which
a high proportion is
illiterate.

**27/The Academy
for Sustainable
Communities**
National training centre,
UK. Designed by Kino
Design, 2004
The ASC is a centre of
excellence established
to develop the skills
needed to deliver the
British government's
Sustainable
Communities housing
programme.

01/

02/

03/

04/

05/

06/

07/

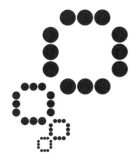

08/

09/

10/

11/

01/Voice
Publishing imprint
focused on women's
issues, USA. Designed
by Eric Baker Design
Associates (CD, D: Eric
Baker), 2006

02/theGlobe.com
Online network of
shared-interest
communities, USA.
Designed by Pentagram
(D: Woody Pirtle), 2001

03/Bravo
Film and arts TV
network, USA. Designed
by Open, 2004

04/Into
Community information
portal, UK. Designed by
Purpose, 2004
Into serves the
community in the
Elephant and Castle
area of south London,
providing access to
information and learning
opportunities, online
and at local centres.

05/Mindjet Corporation
Information visualization
software developer,
USA. Designed by Cahan
& Associates, 2005

06/EVA
Nationwide
communication system,
The Netherlands.
Designed by
ankerxstrijbos, 2003

07/Thinkbox
Marketing body for
TV advertising, UK.
Designed by Kent Lyons,
2006
Persuading advertisers
to go 'on the box'.

08/ebookers.com
Online travel agency,
UK. Designed by Turner
Duckworth, 1998

09/A Clear Idea
Music production
company for TV, film
and commercials, UK.
Designed by Malone
Design (D: David
Malone, Nick Tweedie),
2005

10/Quantel
Visual effects and
editing software
developer, UK. Designed
by Roundel (D: Mike
Denny, John Bateson),
2002

11/The Epilepsy Centre
Charitable association,
Australia. Designed by
Parallax, 2006
A rebranding of the
Epilepsy Association
of South Australia and
Northern Territory that
focuses on the centre's
leadership in lobbying,
raising awareness and
promoting dialogue
about a misunderstood
condition.

01/

02/

03/

04/

05/

MORI ARTS CENTER

06/

07/

08/

Deutsche
Rentenversicherung

Bund

PAP
STAR

09/

10/

11/

01/Pepsi
Soft drink brand, USA.
Designed 1990; modified
1998
Pepsi-Cola, as it was
originally known, first
appeared in 1898
bearing a logotype
with curlicues. This was
sandwiched between
the red and blue waves
in 1950, and replaced in
1962 by an upper-case
logotype. In 1990, the
move was made to a yin
yang-style symbol, with
the logotype outside,
which became the 3D
'Pepsi Globe' in 1998.

02/Scottish Enterprise
Economic development
agency for Scotland, UK.
Designed by Tayburn

**03/Chesapeake
Corporation**
Speciality paperboard
and plastic packaging,
USA. Designed 1964;
updated 2006
This is a refinement
of the company's
original symbol: a 'C'
extended into a wave
of water (representing
Chesapeake Bay)
against a green
(for trees and, more
recently, environmental
stewardship)
background.

04/Farstad Shipping
Supply vessel operator,
Norway. Designer
unknown, 1993

05/Deutsche Börse
Marketplace organizer
and operator of
the Frankfurt Stock
Exchange, Germany.
Designed by Stankowski
& Duschek, 1995

06/SAIC
Carmaker, China.
Designed by Dumbar
Branding, 2006

**07/Japan Nuclear Fuel
Limited**
Reprocessor of spent
nuclear fuel, Japan.
Designed by Katsuichi
Ito Design Studio, 1992

08/Mori Arts Center
Arts and leisure centre,
Japan. Designed by
Jonathan Barnbrook,
2003
Located on the four
top floors of Tokyo's
Roppongi Hills Mori
Tower, Mori Arts Center
includes an art gallery,
an observation deck
and private clubs. Its
logo is a collection of
coloured waveforms,
suggesting a spectrum
of cultural activity. Each
waveform relates to one
of the six constituent
parts of the centre and
serves as a logo in its
own right.

**09/Deutsche
Rentenversicherung**
State pensions scheme,
Germany. Designed by
KMS Team (CD: Christoph
Rohrer, Knut Maierhofer;
D: Bernhard Zölch,
Bruno Marek), 2005
Interlocking fields
express the principle
of solidarity in this
identity for the unified
body of pension
providers to public-
service employees.

10/Pap Star
Disposable paper
products, Germany.
Designed by Stankowski
& Duschek, 1984

**11/Michael Willis
Architects**
Architecture firm, USA.
Designed by Pentagram
(D: Michael Bierut), 2001
Waves spell out
the initials of the
practice and hint at
their commitment to
embracing landscape,
context and the
environment in the
creation of public
buildings and spaces.

12/Coca-Cola
Soft drink brand, USA
Designed by Frank Robinson, 1886; modified by Lippincott Mercer, 1968
Dr John Pemberton, the Atlanta pharmacist who concocted the Coca-Cola formula in a three-legged kettle in his backyard, owed a lot to his bookkeeper, Frank Robinson. It was Robinson who suggested the name for the tonic, which contained extracts of cocaine and the caffeine-rich kola nut. Robinson also scripted the flowing logotype that came to be seen by almost every living soul on the planet. By the late 1960s, however, Robinson's creation had been devalued by careless reproduction in countless colours and backgrounds. The rivalry with Pepsi was intensifying, and the brand was vulnerable. Lippincott Mercer had designed brands for a host of household American names, such as Betty Crocker and Campbells. The firm developed a single, unified, red-and-white expression of the Robinson logotype, which became the corporate identity of the Coca-Cola Company. For the signature soft drink, the words were underlined with the Coca-Cola wave, drawn from the outline of the original bottle. McCann Erickson's immortal slogan, 'It's the real thing', also hails from this time.

13/North Cascades National Bank
Regional bank, USA.
Designed by Fitch
(CD, D: John Rousseau)
Part of NCNB's defence against the threat of big bank brands, this logo combines bold lower-case type with a symbol that implies growth and suggests a bond with the region's mountainous landscape.

14/Meiji Yasuda Life
Life insurance company, Japan. Designed by Bravis International, 2003
Can an insurance company ever appear caring and compassionate? This yin – or yang – shaped cradle has that aim in mind.

15/Dallas/Fort Worth International Airport
International airport, USA. Designed 2001
The 'airstream' lines of this logo represent 'the sense of flight and the freedom that air travel provides the travelling public'. Implementation of the identity commenced just six days before the attacks of 11 September 2001.

16/Massive Music
Music and sound design for commercials and films, The Netherlands. Designed by The Stone Twins, 2001

01/

02/

03/

Ptolemy Mann Woven Textile Art

04/ ....

05/ ....

06/ ....

MILLIKEN®

07/ ....

01/Radiocom
Broadcaster, Romania.
Designed by Brandient,
2005
A new name and visual
identity for Romania's
leading broadcaster,
the National
Radiocommunication
Society, was timed
to anticipate the
company's advance
into telephony and
the Internet.

02/Bank of America
Commercial bank, USA.
Designed by Enterprise
IG (CD: Will Ayres), 2005
The purchase of
BankAmerica by
NationsBank was the
largest bank acquisition
in history at that time.
Unusually, the name of
the combined business
was extrapolated
from that of the
purchased company, as
BankAmerica's history
and status as a national
institution carried
greater weight. Bank
of America's name and
visual identity – stars
and stripes woven
into an agricultural
heartland – were
intended, somewhat
nostalgically, to evoke
'the values that made
banks great in the past'.

03/Morgan Road Books
Publishing imprint, USA.
Designed by Eric Baker
Design Associates
(CD: Eric Baker;
D: Eric Strohl), 2005
Specializing in books
on health, spirituality,
fitness, science and
psychology, Morgan
Road is an imprint of
Random House.

**04/Sentinel Real Estate
Corporation**
Property investment
manager, USA. Designed
by Arnold Saks
Associates, 1988

05/Ptolemy Mann
Woven textile artist, UK.
Designed by Hat-Trick,
2003
Architects and interior
designers are the
market for this artist's
methodically planned
weavings.

**06/Illinois Institute of
Technology**
Science and
engineering university,
USA. Designed 2001
Intersecting 'rays'
symbolize the
integration of disciplines
to create a dynamic
whole.

07/Milliken & Company
Textiles and chemicals
manufacturer, USA.
Designer unknown

brighton and sussex
medical school

01/

02/

03/

BRITISH AIRWAYS

04/

BRUNO GRIZZO

TISHMAN SPEYER

Standard
Chartered

05/

06/

07/

08/ 09/ 10/

11/

01/Brighton and Sussex Medical School
Medical school, UK. Designed by Blast, 2001
This partnership between the universities of Brighton and Sussex combines the teaching and research strengths of each. The DNA-inspired symbol is suggestive of this synergy.

02/AS Communications
Public relations consultancy, UK. Designed by Layfield
The initials stand for PR consultant Alistair Smith, and their straight lines represent lines of communication.

03/Hmmm
National schools campaign to promote careers in the arts, UK. Designed by SomeOne, 2004

04/British Airways
International airline, UK. Designed by Newell & Sorrell, 1997
The BA ribbon is a distant echo of the 'Speedbird' symbol first used by Imperial Airways in 1932 and then by BOAC. On aircraft, the ribbon was originally accompanied by BA's short-lived 'ethnic art' tailfins, which were famously rubbished by former Prime Minister Margaret Thatcher. She draped her handkerchief over a model BA aircraft at

the 1997 Conservative Party Conference, declaring, 'We fly the British flag, not these awful things'. The tailfins were hurriedly repainted with a Union Flag design based on one first used on Concorde.

05/Bruno Grizzo
Womenswear label, USA. Designed by Matthias Ernstberger, 2006

06/Tishman Speyer
Property owner, developer and investor, USA. Designed by Doyle Partners, 2006

07/Standard Chartered
International banking group, UK. Designed by Enterprise IG, 2003

08/Invista
Integrated polymers and fibres group, USA. Designed by Enterprise IG (CD: Judy Viglietti), 2002
Branding for a newly independent group of DuPont companies, with added 'rings of innovation'.

09/University of Dundee Exhibitions Department
Contemporary art galleries, events and resources, UK. Designed by Sarah Tripp, 2003

10/Physicians Mutual
Insurance provider, USA. Designed by Siegel & Gale, 2004

11/Woolmark
Quality endorsement mark for The Woolmark Company, Australia. Designed by Francesco Saroglia, 1964
The need for a single universal image for wool quality was the driving force behind the creation of the Woolmark. Nowadays, it commands global consumer confidence. In 1997, the International Wool Secretariat changed its name to The Woolmark Company to associate its corporate identity more closely with the brand. (Reproduced with the permission of The Woolmark Company.)

orchardcentral

Double Knot℗

12/Mind
Mental health charity, UK
Designed by Glazer, 2004
Up until quite recently in the UK it would have
been considered the height of extravagance, if
not an outright waste of hard-earned funds, for a
charity to commission a professional rebranding
programme of the kind usually undertaken by
major businesses. But competition for funds, hearts
and minds has grown so intense that charities
have been left little choice. For the most part
they have been rewarded, and their investment
in consultancy fees and implementation can be
justified to their supporters. When Mind rebranded,
its annual donations leapt from £8 million to £17
million, and it emerged as the 'spokesbody' for the
mental healthcare industry. The identity unified 200
affiliated charities in England and Wales, plus a
range of other divisions, and established a single
consistent voice for the organization. At its centre
was the new Mind logo, which, in just a handwritten
scribble and word, elegantly conveys the image of
an organization seeking compassionate solutions
to complex and challenging problems.

13/Orchard Central
Retail development,
Singapore. Designed
by Fitch, 2006
A dynamic mark,
in which the line
reconfigures itself
endlessly, reflects
a lively shopping
experience.

14/Double Knot
Music video production
company, UK. Designed
by Stylo Design (AD,
D: Tom Lancaster), 2004
The two founding
members tie up the
end of this logo.

01/

02/

03/

Prison
Radio
Association

IMPERIAL WAR

MUSEUM

01/Nikon
Optics and imaging
equipment group,
Japan. Designed 2003
The rays of light that
decorate Nikon's well-
known black logotype
represent the future and
the possibilities therein.

02/Scope
Fundraising body for
film projects, Belgium.
Designed by HGV, 2005

03/British Film Institute
Institute for the
promotion of film
culture, UK. Designed by
Johnson Banks, 2006
As the range of BFI
activities widened, the
institute's old identity
was lost. A cinematic
lens flare puts the BFI
back in the spotlight.

04/Lou Reed Music
Record label, USA.
Designed by
Sagmeister Inc
(CD: Stefan Sagmeister;
AD, D: Matthias
Ernstberger), 2002
A valve from one of Lou
Reed's favourite vintage
amplifiers provides the
visual identity for his
record company.

05/Lighthouse
Professional
development body for
film industry creatives,
UK. Designed by Kino
Design, 2006

06/VJ Launch
Veejay and video
artists' showcase, The
Netherlands. Designed
by ankerxstrijbos, 2005
An identity for a project
by Utrecht's Hogeschool
voor de Kunsten and
Centraal Museum, in
which young veejays
and video artists
perform for large
audiences.

07/Taiyo Mutual
Life insurance provider,
Japan. Designed by
Bravis International,
1997
Like many Japanese
insurance firms, Taiyo
sells its products
through a network of
saleswomen, to women.
The sun's reflection in
water was chosen as a
more feminine image for
the company instead
of the more traditional
symbol of a rising sun
('taiyo' means 'sun').

**08/Prison Radio
Association**
Support for prison
and community
broadcasters, UK.
Designed by Dave and
Jamie (D: Jamie Ellul,
David Azurdia), 2006
Like swords to
ploughshares, the
prison bars (or the
marking of time on
a cell wall) become
broadcast sound.

**09/Imperial War
Museum**
Museum of wartime
culture, UK. Designed by
Minale Tattersfield
(AD: Brian Tattersfield;
D: Paul Astbury), 1995
Searchlights describe
the 'W' and 'M' and
illuminate land, sea
and air.

Surefire

02/

03/

04/

05/

06/

07/

01/Dutch Police Force
National police authority, The Netherlands
Designed by Studio Dumbar, 1993
In the late 1980s, Gert Dumbar's studio was the standard-bearer for a vibrant new wave of Dutch design, characterized by striking staged photography and anarchic typography. It was a brave step by The Netherlands' Ministry of the Interior and Ministry of Justice to appoint the studio to design a completely fresh identity for the newly merged national and municipal police forces. The logo had to satisfy two forces, each with their own proud heraldic emblem: the flaming grenade of the national police and the weighty law book of the municipal force. Stripping these of their militaristic pomp and fusing them into a single abstract form within the word 'Politie' created a mark that balanced progressiveness with authority. The predictable public outcry over the highly conspicuous orange, red and blue diagonal striping of police vehicles soon faded, and the identity system is now a source of national pride.

02/Surefire
Media training consultancy, UK.
Designed by Stylo Design (AD, D: Tom Lancaster), 2003
Look for the 'S' in the flames of the fire.

03/Radio Free Europe/ Radio Liberty
Pro-democracy radio station, USA. Designed by Chermayeff & Geismar Inc. (D: Steff Geissbuhler, Sagi Haviv), 2004
RFE/RL is a private broadcaster in the region of eastern and south-eastern Europe, Russia, the Caucasus, central and south-west Asia and the Middle East, funded by the US Congress.

04/38 Walton Street Gas
Gas and heating engineers, UK. Designed by Sam Dallyn, 2003

05/Amnesty International
Human rights movement, UK. Designed by Diana Redhouse, 1961
Amnesty's powerful and enduring symbol of a candle wrapped in barbed wire was the brainchild of the organization's founder, Peter Benenson. When briefing artist Diana Redhouse, Benenson recalled the ancient Chinese proverb: 'Better to light a candle than curse the darkness'.

06/Musée d'Art et d'Histoire de Judaïsme
Museum of Jewish art and history, France. Designed by Studio Apeloig, 1997

07/British Gas
Domestic energy supplier, UK. Designed by Coley Porter Bell, 1997

01/

02/ 03/ 04/

05/

ASSURANT

06/ 07/ 08/

 Sony Ericsson

09/

01/Konica Minolta
Imaging equipment manufacturer, Japan. Designed by Saul Bass, 1978; new logotype designed by Konica Minolta, 2003
The mark designed by Saul Bass was for Minolta, which later merged with Konica. According to the 2003 announcement of the revised mark, the symbol is a representation of earth, while the five lines 'represent light beams and express our wide-ranging technological expertise in the field of imaging'.

02/Total
Oil and gas company, France. Designed by A & Co (D: Laurent Vincenti), 2003
According to designer Vincenti, the mark 'drew itself one night when I couldn't sleep', and is intended to bring to mind energy streams (heat, light and movement).

03/Carat
International media agency network, UK. Designed by North Design, 2003
Seen on the company's website, the mobile colour-changing bubble is Carat's 'media sphere' and represents the movement of ideas in global media.

04/AT&T
Telecommunications provider, USA. Designed by Bass/Yager (D: Saul Bass), 1983; modified by Interbrand, 2005
In 1983, Saul Bass designed a globe for AT&T to symbolize its international network and vision. It became one of the USA's favourite logos, and led to the brand receiving a 98% awareness rating. When AT&T merged with SBC, the AT&T name was kept but its mark was evolved to 'signal its new, additional reach' and 'make the brand more approachable'.

05/Symantec
Internet security technology, USA. Designed by Interbrand, 2001

06/Kenmore Property Group
Property investment and development group, UK. Designed by Navyblue Design Group (D: Richie Hartness), 2006

07/Nortel
Telecommunications equipment manufacturer, USA. Designed by Siegel & Gale, 1995

08/Assurant
Insurance group, USA. Designed by Carbone Smolan Agency, 2004
In 2004, the USA businesses of the Fortis Group were combined in a single group, named Assurant, and sold in one of the biggest initial public offerings of that year. A loosely woven globe expressed the group's new fabric of skills and specialities.

09/Sony Ericsson
Mobile communications equipment, UK. Designed 2001
Sony Ericsson's 'liquid' logo could be construed as an 's' or an 'e', an egg, an eyeball or a pulsating green heart. It has featured in advertising campaigns (devised by Wolff Olins) in the role of a ♥ symbol, for example: 'I (liquid logo) making it happen'.

Continental Airlines

SETI Institute

11/

12/

13/

Friends of the Earth

14/

10/BT
Communications group, UK
Designed by Wolff Olins, 1998; implemented as BT corporate identity, 2003
BT's evolution from a public utility to a group providing communications services in 170 countries can be charted through three logos. The first, designed by Banks & Miles to signal the pre-privatization renaming of Post Office Telecommunications as British Telecom in 1980, featured a partially dotted technological 'T' that presented the utility in a completely fresh light. Wolff Olins's multicultural 'piper' of 1991 blew the trumpet for a new, truncated trading name – BT – whose rootlessness was designed to pave the way for international alliances and expansion. The piper's pose of one hand to its ear and the other on its pan pipes symbolized communication but drew comparisons with fairies. The piper stayed the course, though, until 2003 when a new BT management team, wishing to launch a new set of strategic priorities and 'behavioural values', latched onto a symbol originally designed by Wolff Olins in 1998. It had been rejected then, but was used to brand BTopenworld (an Internet service) in 2000 before being rolled out as the group's new corporate mark in 2003.

11/Continental Airlines
International airline, USA. Designed by Lippincott Mercer, 1991
The partial globe replaced the jet-stream symbol designed in 1968 by Saul Bass to reflect the company's emergence as one of the world's most widely travelling airlines.

12/Saturn
Electrical appliances retailer, Germany. Designed by KMS Team (CD: Knut Maierhofer; D: Bruno Marek, Peta Kobrow), 1999

13/SETI Institute
Space research institute, USA. Designed by Turner Duckworth, 1998
SETI stands for 'Search for Extraterrestrial Intelligence', but the work of this private non-profit organization includes scientific and educational projects 'relevant to the origin, nature, prevalence and distribution of life in the universe'. It is complex work, a fact not reflected by SETI's previous logo of a radar dish against a night sky.

14/Friends of the Earth
Environmental network, USA. Designed 2001

STAR ALLIANCE™

01/

02/

03/

04/

05/

06/

07/

08/

09/

10/

11/

01/Epcor
Power and water
supplier, Canada.
Designed 1999
Epcor's name is derived
from Edmonton Power
Corporation. Owned by
the City of Edmonton,
the company provides
energy and water
to Alberta, British
Columbia, Ontario
and the USA Pacific
Northwest.

02/Star Alliance
Global airline network,
Germany. Designed by
Pentagram (D: Justus
Oehler), 2001
The five elements
represent the five
founding member
airlines of the alliance.

03/Stella Bianca
Hand tool manufacturer,
Italy. Designed by
Brunazzi Associati
(D: Andrea Brunazzi),
2005

04/Auction My Stuff
Charitable online
auction agent, UK.
Designed by Corporate
Edge, 2006
Notting Hill Housing
Trust needed an identity
for its arm that sells
unwanted items on
eBay in return for a 30%
commission, which goes
to charity.

05/USA Canoe/Kayak
National canoe and
kayak team, USA.
Designed by Crosby
Associates, 1988
'A' for America, a fin
slicing through water, a
star and stripes: it's all
covered here.

**06/Columbus Regional
Hospital**
Hospital, USA. Designed
by Pentagram (D:
Michael Gericke), 1991
A major hospital in
south-east Indiana, CRH
adopts the rising sun of
the state's traditional
seal as its own emblem.

07/SunTrust Banks
Financial services
group, USA. Designed
by Siegel & Gale, 2004

08/Multicanal
Latin American cable TV
provider, Argentina.
Designed by Chermayeff
& Geissbuhler, 1996
Multicanal's multiple
channels – and,
implicitly, top-quality
service – are symbolized
by five stars, which also
create an 'M'.

09/Raeta Estates
Residential property
development, USA.
Designed by Design
Ranch (AD: Michelle
Sonderegger, Ingred
Sidie; D: Tad Carpenter),
2005
A rural Kansas
development wanted
to impart the feel of a
rancher's brand, where
the lots are big, the
views are grand and
the properties take their
names from characters
in the movie 'Giant'.

10/Outposts
Outdoor adventure
specialist, UK. Designed
by Mytton Williams
(D: Bob Mytton), 2006

11/Canal 13
TV network, Argentina.
Designed by Chermayeff
& Geissbuhler (D: Steff
Geissbuhler), 1993

Mercedes-Benz

13/

14/

15/

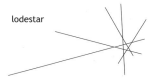

lodestar

heavenly™

16/

17/

18/

12/Mercedes-Benz
Vehicle manufacturer, Germany
Designed 1909; modified 1916, 1937
The name Mercedes and the symbol of a star
came together by complete chance. Emil Jellinek,
an aristocrat who sold Daimlers to friends in
high society, also raced the vehicles under the
pseudonym of his daughter's name, Mercédès. His
orders were vital to the Cannstadt factory, and in
1900 it was decided to make Mercedes the trade
name for the cars. Also wanting a symbol, Paul and
Adolf Daimler recalled the significance of the star in
the career of their father and the company founder,
Gottlieb. Starting work at the Deutz gas engine
factory, the young engineer had sent a postcard of
the town to his wife, marking his house with a star.
One day, he wrote, a star would shine over his own
factory. A three-pointed star was registered in 1909.
It was enclosed by a ring in 1916 and, when Daimler
merged with rival Benz in 1926, the latter's laurel
leaves and the name Mercedes-Benz encircled the
star. In 1937, the logo with a plain ring was seen for
the first time.

13/Texaco
Oil company, USA
Designed 1981; modified
2000
After almost 20 years of
Texaco's streamlined
star, the company had
enough confidence in
the public's recognition
of its identity to do
away with the logotype
altogether, leaving the
mark to function on
its own.

14/Ohio National
Life insurance company,
USA. Designed by
Pentagram (D: Michael
Bierut), 1996
Ohio's state seal
features a sun rising
beyond a mountainous
horizon and inspired
this logo.

15/Hotel Caleta
Hotel, Mexico.
Designed by Lance
Wyman, 1969

16/Lodestar
Business consultancy,
Australia. Designed by
Coast Design, 2001

17/BrandMD
Branding agency for
medical practices, USA.
Designed by Moon
Brand (D: Peter Dean),
2006
The identity combines
notions of first aid (the
red cross), medical
services (the 'star of life'
used mainly in the USA
by emergency services)
and noteworthiness
(the asterisk).

18/Heavenly Wine
Online wine merchant,
UK. Designed by
Turner Duckworth
(CD: David Turner,
Bruce Duckworth;
D: Sam Lachlan), 2005

01/

02/

Aer Lingus

03/

04/

05/

TORONTO
BOTANICAL
GARDEN

01/Linden78
Apartment development, USA. Designed by G2 (D: Pablo Pineda, Jason Borzouyeh), 2006
Corcoran's condominium development, Linden78, is situated on the linden-tree-lined West 78th Street, Manhattan, overlooking Central Park.

02/LA21
Landscape architects and planners, Germany. Designed by Thomas Manss & Company, 2005
The foliage/fountain suggests the varied scale and formality of projects undertaken by LA21.

03/Aer Lingus
International airline, Ireland. Designed 1996
Aer Lingus is an anglicized form of the Irish for 'air fleet', 'Aer Loingeas'. The traditional Irish symbol of a shamrock first appeared on tailfins in 1965.

04/Losada
Spanish-language publishing house, Spain. Designed by Pentagram (D: Fernando Gutierrez), 2002
A move to Spain for this long-established Argentinian publisher prompted a new logo and look for its back catalogue to attract a broader cross-section of readers.

05/Air Canada
International airline, Canada. Designed 2004
Air Canada's maple leaf has been around since the days when it was known as Trans-Canada Airlines.

06/Toronto Botanical Garden
Volunteer-based horticultural information centre, Canada. Designed by Hambly & Woolley (CD: Bob Hambly; DD: Barb Woolley; D: Emese Ungar-Walker), 2004

07/Target Archer Farms
Premium food brand, USA. Designed by Templin Brink Design (CD: Joel Templin, Gaby Brink; D: Brian Gunderson), 2003

08/Mitea Rare Teas
Tea importer, USA. Designed by Segura Inc, 1996

09/adidas Sport Heritage
Heritage sportswear manufacturer, Germany. Designed 1971
In creating his three-stripes branding, first used on sports shoes in 1949 and on clothes in 1967, founder Adi Dassler was decades ahead of other sports marketers. In the late 1960s, he sought a new mark that could spearhead the expansion into clothing and leisure. From a pool of over 100 ideas, the trefoil was chosen, featuring three geometric segments or leaves that expressed the new diversity of the adidas brand. It was first seen on products in 1972, went on to became the company's corporate mark and is now the logo for its 'heritage' product division.

10/

11/

12/

THE NATIONAL TRUST

13/

THE ORCHARD

14/

15/

16/

CHELSEA GARDEN CENTER

ngs

10/Fully Loaded Tea
Whole-leaf and fruit tea producer, Canada. Designed by Subplot Design (CD: Matthew Clark, Roy White), 2006

11/US Green Building Council
Construction industry coalition for environmentally responsible buildings, USA. Designed by Doyle Partners

12/Wave Hill
Public garden and cultural centre, USA. Designed by Pentagram (D: David Hillman), 1996
With 28 acres of lush gardens and woodland, this centre brings nature and environmental education to the Bronx.

13/The National Trust
Historic property conservation charity, UK. Designed 1935; modified by David Gentleman, 1980s
The familiar NT oak-leaf symbol was originally conceived in 1935 as a result of a national design competition. When one of the UK's leading illustrators, David Gentleman, re-drew it, he added a second acorn to celebrate the trust's membership reaching two million. Despite having now passed the three-million mark, the trust has stuck with two acorns.

14/Brooklyn Botanic Garden
Urban botanic garden, USA. Designed by Carbone Smolan Agency
As well as suggesting diversity and transformation, the sculptural image reflects the garden's policy of showing plant life as works of art.

15/Ulmer
Scientific publisher, Germany. Designed by MetaDesign, 2004
A stylized elm leaf represents a scientific publisher wishing to project a fresher, more accessible image.

16/The Orchard
Sydney bar/restaurant, Australia. Designed by Layfield, 2006

17/Chelsea Garden Center
Gardening retailer, USA. Designed by C&G Partners (D: Justine Gaxotte), 2005

18/National Gardens Scheme
Scheme opening private gardens to the public for charity, UK. Designed by Roundel (D: John Bateson, Andy Hills), 2004

hilliard

01/

AMERICAN
GREETINGS

02/

MAYFLOWER
Inn & Spa

03/

mayfair flowers

04/

05/

RoyalVanZanten
surprising nature

essential pictures

06/   07/   08/

SINCE 2004

Drugstore

TALENT
MANAGEMENT

09/

01/Hilliard
'Gastro café', UK.
Designed by Spin, 2004
Four petals represent
the seasonal produce
on sale at this café
close to St Paul's
Cathedral.

02/American Greetings
Greeting card
manufacturer, USA.
Designed by Lippincott
Mercer, 1978

03/Mayflower Inn & Spa
Country house inn and
spa, USA. Designed
by Eric Baker Design
Associates (CD: Eric
Baker; D: Eric Strohl),
2005

04/Mayfair Flowers
Flower-arranging
school, Japan.
Designed by Taste Inc
(D: Toshiyasu Nanbu,
Masaaki Miyara), 2005

05/Dixie
Paper cup
manufacturer, USA.
Designed by Saul Bass,
1969

06/Royal Van Zanten
Flower producer, The
Netherlands. Designed
by Total Identity
(SD: André Mol), 2001

07/Design Heroine
Architecture practice,
UK. Designed by Value
and Service, 2005
Design Heroine
was established by
Harriet Harriss and
Suzi Winstanley, two
researchers who met at
the Royal College of Art.
The broken flower was
chosen as a contrast
to the firm's overtly
feminine name.

08/Essential Pictures
Nature and flower
photography, The
Netherlands. Designed
by Tel Design (D: Jaco
Emmen), 2004

09/Drugstore
Talent management
agency, UK.
Designed by Arthur-
SteenHorneAdamson,
2005
An identity that draws
an analogy between the
selection and sourcing
of creative teams and
the 'one-stop shop'
of the early American
drugstore, which sold all
manner of goods from
tobacco and candy to
toiletries and medicine.

10/

11/

12/

keep
Indianapolis
beautiful ᴵ ᴺ ᶜ.

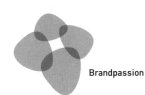

Brandpassion

AMANDA
LACEY
LONDON

The Rose
Bankside's
First Theatre

10/Labour Party
Political party, UK.
Designed by Michael
Wolff, 1986
The decision to switch
from a flaglike logotype
to a red rose was taken
by the then-leader of
the party, Neil Kinnock,
and launched at the
1986 Labour conference.
New Labour's solid red
square logo elbowed
the rose from the
front line, but it is still
in use and remains a
memorable piece of
political symbolism.

11/De Ruiter
Rose breeder, The
Netherlands. Designed
by Total Identity
(SD: André Mol), 2005

**12/Environmental
Protection Agency**
Regulatory and
research agency, USA.
Designed by Chermayeff
& Geismar Inc. (D: Steff
Geissbuhler), 1978

**13/Keep Indianapolis
Beautiful Inc.**
Not-for-profit urban
renewal agency, USA.
Designed by Lodge
Design (D: Eric Kass),
2005

14/Brandpassion
Fashion industry
branding consultancy,
Denmark. Designed by
Bysted, 2002

15/Amanda Lacey
Skincare treatments, UK.
Designed by SomeOne
(D: Laura Hussey, Simon
Manchipp, David Law,
Kam Tang), 2006
Skincare expert to
the stars, Amanda
Lacey brought out a
range of products and
accessories in 2006
branded with a flower,
each petal of which was
Lacey's profile.

16/The Rose
Theatre museum, UK.
Designed by NB: Studio
(AD: Nick Finney, Ben
Stott, Alan Dye), 1999
Plans are afoot to
excavate the remaining
foundations of The Rose
– the first purpose-built
theatre on London's
Bankside, built in 1587 –
to create a permanent
exhibition on the
site. The phoenix-
like ambition of the
enterprise is captured
by its logo, with the
original building
sprouting a flourishing
Tudor rose.

Campaign to Protect
Rural England

g a d a l a i k i

Conservatives

08/   09/   10/

THE PARK

11/

01/Andrus Children's Center
Children's care and learning centre, USA. Designed by Chermayeff & Geismar Inc. (D: Steff Geissbuhler, Henricus Kusbiantoro), 1999

02/Royal Tropical Institute
Centre for international and intercultural cooperation, The Netherlands. Designed by Eden, 2006
A tree of life reflects the global focus of this not-for-profit organization.

03/Trees For Cities
Ecological charity, UK. Designed by Atelier Works, 1998
Thumbprints on a tower block represent the power of collective action for Trees for Cities, which encourages local communities to plant trees to reverse decades of damage done by neglect and poor architecture.

04/The Young Foundation
Centre for social innovation, UK. Designed by Pentagram (D: Justus Oehler), 2005
A symbol that expresses the hope of finding new ways to meet pressing needs in British society.

05/Neal's Yard
Natural remedies, UK. Designed by Turner Duckworth, 2001
Designed to distance Neal's Yard from its poorer quality imitators, the identity creates a quality 'seal' that depicts the source (plant extracts) of its products.

06/Tram
Athens tramway system, Greece. Designed by HGV, 2002
Notorious for its air pollution, Athens introduced a new tramway system to welcome visitors to the 2002 Olympic Games. Its identity makes explicit the environmental advantage of taking the tram.

07/Greater Rochester Orthopaedics
Orthopaedic practice, USA. Designed by Moon Brand (D: Richard Moon, Peter Dean), 2003
The 'Tree of Andry' is a common symbol for orthopaedic practices. Andry was the author of a 1741 book that contained an illustration of a young tree with a crooked trunk: a demonstration that bone is not inert matter, but living tissue. For this upstate New York practice, the 'R' made the perfect tree trunk.

08/Campaign to Protect Rural England
Charity for preserving the English countryside, UK. Designed by Pentagram (D: John McConnell), 2003

09/Gadalaiki
Holiday village, Latvia. Designed by Zoom, 2006
'Gadalaiki' is Latvian for 'seasons'.

10/Conservative Party
Political party, UK. Designed by Perfect Day, 2006
Replacing the strident Thatcher-era flaming torch, the new emblem is designed to associate the party with renewal, growth and the environment. It got the party faithful up in arms, and prompted Bernard Ingham, Margaret Thatcher's former press secretary, to suggest that the party had gone 'completely mad'.

11/The Park
Italian restaurant, UK. Designed by Dew Gibbons, 1998

01/

02/

03/

04/

Münchner
Stadtentwässerung

05/

 First Choice

 the people's valley

RiverSource  SM

06/   07/   08/

Alpine Oral Surgery

09/

01/Dura Vermeer
Construction contractor and developer, The Netherlands. Designed by Tel Design (D: Eegène Heijblom, Edwin van Praet), 2000

02/Amtrak
National intercity passenger rail service, USA. Designed by OH&Co, 2000
Despite still being owned by the federal government, Amtrak decided that its 1971 'inverted arrow' identity (designed by Lippincott & Margulies) represented 'a different kind of institution' in 2000. The new logo conveys the pleasure of train travel as part of Amtrak's bid to convert more people to rail,

and was launched at Los Angeles' Union Station at the same time as the company's Unconditional Satisfaction Guarantee.

03/Lake Hills Church
Austin, Texas church, USA. Designed by Marc English Design, 2000

04/Lake Placid Film Forum
Annual film festival, USA. Designed by Eric Baker Design Associates (CD: Eric Baker; D: Eric Strohl), 2003

05/Münchner Stadtentwässerung
Municipal water services, Germany. Designed by Büro für Gestaltung Wangler & Abele, 2004
A symbol that suggests the environment – water, landscape, sky – or, interpreted another way, water ripples seen through a circle representing the scope of the agency's activities (tube, channel and reservoir).

06/First Choice
Travel agency chain, UK. Designed by Enterprise IG, 1999
The colour and innocence of this symbol is balanced by the more serious and 'professional' logotype. It set a trend in the travel industry, where, until quite recently, logos were a good deal duller.

07/The People's Valley
Interactive marketing agency, The Netherlands. Designed by ankerxstrijbos, 2005

08/RiverSource
Investments, insurance and annuities provider, USA. Designed by Lippincott Mercer, 2006

09/Alpine Oral Surgery
Oral surgical centre, USA. Designed by BBK Studio, 2003

11/

12/

13/

14/

10/Celebration
Planned community, USA
Designed by Pentagram (D: Michael Bierut), 1993–97
Identity design is, for the most part, a business of smoke and mirrors. Logos create illusions; they seek to conceal imperfections and satisfy our longing for the ideal. In the case of Celebration, the town built from scratch by the Walt Disney Company in the Florida swampland, the illusion extends far beyond the logo. It encompasses the entire community, from its brand new Revival-style houses to the picket fences, metal street signs and 1950s-inspired movie house. A community that suggests a mythical, misty, sweet-as-apple-pie version of life in small-town postwar America, Celebration was the realization of the long-held Disney dream of building an experimental model town for the future. Michael Bierut's team at Pentagram played a central role in its creation, designing street signs, ironmongery and identities for the town's golf club, hospital, cinema and office buildings. All the logo, or town 'seal', had to do was play along with the illusion. The logo design was one of many put forward for the town's manhole covers, but was picked out by the client and given an elevated role. As a logo, it does the rare thing of truthfully reflecting reality – even if the reality is a dream.

11/CanaVialis
Genetic improvers of sugarcane, Brazil. Designed by FutureBrand BC&H, 2003

12/Prudential Financial
Insurance, financial and property services, USA. Designed 1890s; updated by Siegel & Gale, 1990
One of the longest lasting and most familiar marks in American corporate history, the Rock of Gibraltar was chosen for its associations with strength and security.

13/Manomet Center for Conservation Sciences
Environmental research centre, USA. Designed by Malcolm Grear Designers, 1992

14/Landform
Property developer, UK. Designed by Spin, 2005
Multiple abstract images suggest the shaping and sculpting of the environment.

01/

PIPERLIME

02/

03/

04/

05/

smile

06/ ⋯⋯⋯⋯⋯ 07/ ⋯⋯⋯⋯⋯ 08/ ⋯⋯⋯⋯⋯

 kidfresh

09/ ⋯⋯⋯⋯⋯

01/Talentum
Professional journals and online content service, Finland. Designed 2002

02/FourStories
Advertising agency, USA. Designed by Bob Dinetz Design, 2004 Based in Portland, Oregon, this is an ad agency with a difference: a business model based on only having four clients at any one time. The eight empty places in the egg box indicate a capacity to take on more work and, by implication, a reluctance to do so if it means the firm's attention will be diverted from its current accounts.

03/Piperlime
Online shoe retailer, USA. Designed by Pentagram (AD: Brian Jacobs; D: Rob Duncan), 2006

04/Ingreedyents
Online supplier of food from growers, UK. Designed by Airside, 2006

05/Apple
Consumer electronics manufacturer, USA. Designed by Regis McKenna Advertising (D: Rob Janoff), 1977; updated 1999
The first Apple logo, created by company co-founder Ron Wayne, was a Gothic-style depiction of Sir Isaac Newton seated under an apple tree wreathed by

a banner announcing 'Apple Computer Inc'. Hired by Steve Jobs to come up with something that could reproduce more clearly, young art director Rob Janoff began with a silhouette of an apple, but felt it looked too much like a cherry tomato. A bite from the side added a sense of scale and was seen as a play on 'byte'. Jobs asked for rainbow stripes to advertise the colour screen of the Apple II, and an icon of the computer age was born. In 1999, the stripes disappeared, leaving just an instantly recognizable shape.

06/Scott Howard
Gourmet restaurant, USA. Designed by Turner Duckworth (AD: David Turner, Bruce Duckworth; D: David Turner, Jonathan Warner), 2005
Chef Scott Howard creates California-French dishes with local seasonal ingredients. A carrot-cum-arrow points the way to a high-precision lunch or dinner.

07/Smile
Dental health practice, UK. Designed by Hat-Trick, 2001
Dental practices have to work hard to make themselves attractive to the public. This high-street practice succeeded by choosing a name and logo that focuses on the positive health and prevention messages of dentistry.

08/Tomato
Mobile phone network, Croatia. Designed by Büro X (AD: Andreas Miedaner; D: Werner Singer), 2006

09/Kidfresh
Organic prepared children's meals, USA. Designed by Addis Creson, 2005

01/

02/

03/

INDIANAPOLIS ZOO

SEA HORSES

one fish two fish

01/Dutch Cancer Society
Cancer research and
education charity, The
Netherlands. Designed
by Tel Design (D: Jaco
Emmen, Annemieke
Later, Pieter van
Rosmalen), 2004
Cancer the disease, like
its namesake star sign,
is symbolized by a crab.
Both can exert a fierce
grip, but the connection
is through the Latin word
'cancer', which meant
both 'gangrene' and
'crab'.

02/Vancouver Aquarium
Marine science centre,
Canada. Designed by
Subplot Design
(CD: Matthew Clark,
Roy White), 2006
For more than 35 years
the aquarium's main
emblem was a killer
whale; it was one of
the first institutions
to display one. The
whale was replaced
by a leaping fish made
up of aquatic fauna
(starfish), flora (kelp)
and water (wave) to
mark the centre's 50th
anniversary and to
embody a commitment
to the conservation of
all aquatic life rather
than one or two species.

03/Dolphin Square
Property development,
UK. Designed by Ico
Design, 2006
An identity for the
newly refurbished 1930s
riverside apartment
complex in Pimlico,
south-west London.

04/Seahorses
Permanent exhibit at
Indianapolis Zoo, USA.
Designed by Lodge
Design, 2005

05/One Fish Two Fish
Childrenswear and
maternitywear retailer,
Australia. Designed by
Naughtyfish Design,
2003

2.31 Winged
insects

01/

02/

03/

04/ .... 05/ .... 06/ ....

07/ ....

01/British Bee Society
Charity, UK. Designed by Peter Grundy, 1995

02/MSN
Internet services group, USA. Designed by FutureBrand, 2000
Microsoft's collection of Internet services was launched in 1995 as MSN (Microsoft Network). It dovetailed with the launch of Windows 95, which included features to improve access to Web material. However, MSN's content, which made use of multimedia, animations and interactive features, alienated users with low-capacity PCs and dial-up connections. In 2000, MSN relaunched as a more traditional Internet service provider

with a fresh colourful identity. The butterfly could be attached to any kind of service, from email, messaging and online communities to shopping, games and personal finance. Subscriptions have risen to 9 million and, in late 2006, msn.com had the second highest traffic of any website.

03/Papalote Children's Museum
Children's museum, Mexico. Designed by Lance Wyman, 1991
'Papalote' means 'kite' in Spanish, and 'papálotl' is 'butterfly' in the Aztec Nahuatl language. The shapes in the wings suggest the museum's geometric buildings.

04/Ability International
Accessibility charity, UK. Designed by Thomas Manss & Company, 1997
Ability International works to increase access to mainstream leisure activities for disabled and disadvantaged members of society. Its symbol represents the freedom and helping hand it offers to people with special needs and those close to them.

05/Papillon Cakes
Pastry and cake designer, Canada. Designed by Hambly & Woolley (CD: Bob Hambly; DD: Barb Woolley; D: Frances Chen), 2006

06/Ciba Speciality Chemicals
Chemicals manufacturer, Switzerland. Designed by Gottschalk & Ash, 1996
In 1996, Ciba-Geigy, one of the world's largest chemical and biological groups, merged with the pharmaceutical company Sandoz to create Novartis, the life sciences group. Almost immediately, the speciality chemical divisions were spun off in the world's largest demerger, and launched in 117 countries under the Ciba name. The creature that took flight came in four colours, one for each division of the business.

07/Mosquito
Record label, UK. Designed by Sam Dallyn, 2003
Mosquito's specialist interest in 'minimal' dance music is reflected in its identity: a creature that, despite its lack of stature, is still hard to ignore.

01/

02/

03/

04/

05/

06/

07/

08/

09/

10/

11/

01/Hanaro
Telecommunications
services, South Korea.
Designed by Total
Identity (D: Aad van
Dommelen, André Mol),
2004

02/The White Swan
Public house, UK.
Designed by SomeOne
(D: David Law, Simon
Manchipp), 2005

03/Erskine
Regeneration marketing
consultancy, UK.
Designed by Funnel
Creative, 2005
The early bird catching
the worm becomes
a metaphor for new
business development.

04/NBC
TV network, USA.
Designed by Chermayeff
& Geismar Inc. (D: Steff
Geissbuhler), 1986
Apart from a three-
year period in the 1970s
when NBC adopted
a stylized 'N' symbol
with disastrous results
(Nebraska ETV Network
successfully sued for
trademark infringement),
the peacock with
multicoloured plumage
has been a fixture
since 1956. In 1986, its
number of feathers was
trimmed from eleven to
six (representing NBC's
six divisions), and its
head turned in a more
forward-looking pose.
Along with Tweety Pie
and Woody Woodpecker
it is one of the world's
best-known birds.

05/Penelope
Stylist, UK. Designed by
SomeOne, 2006
A magpie represents this
stylist with an eye for
beautiful things.

**06/United States
Institute of Peace**
Independent peace-
building institution, USA.
Designed by Malcolm
Grear Designers, 1990
A dove (with olive
branch) flies over the
Connecticut 'Peace
Tree', which was used
by the Suckiauke
Indians as a site for
peace councils and also
provided a hiding place
for the colonists' charter
of liberty when they
were seeking freedom
from Britain.

07/Bluebird Café
Kansas City vegetarian
restaurant, USA.
Designed by Design
Ranch (AD, D: Michelle
Sonderegger, Ingred
Sidie), 2004

08/Acuere
Business software
developer, Australia.
Designed by Parallax,
2004

09/Mazda
Car manufacturer,
Japan. Designed 1997
Mazda's 1997 'M' symbol
features a central 'V'
that is 'symbolic of the
company stretching its
wings as it soars into
the future'.

**10/Washington
Convention Center**
Conference centre, USA.
Designed by Lance
Wyman, 1979
An identity that reflects
the architecture of
the centre.

11/Penguin
Publishing house, UK.
Designed by Edward
Young, 1935; modified
by Jan Tschichold, 1946,
and Pentagram (D:
Angus Hyland), 2005
Allen Lane, founder
of Penguin, wanted a
'dignified but flippant'
symbol for his new line
of paperbacks. His
secretary suggested
a penguin and Lane
dispatched office
junior Edward Young
to London Zoo to make
some sketches. His

lifelike but lumpen bird
was redrawn by master
typographer Tschichold
and given its defining
one-eyed sideways
glance.

13/

14/

15/

16/

12/Lufthansa
International airline, Germany
Designed by Otto Firle, 1918; modified by Otl Aicher, 1969
The Lufthansa crane occupies a hallowed position in the history of corporate identity. The stylized bird in flight symbolizes flying and technical skills and was created by Professor Otto Firle for the first German airline Deutsche Luftreederei GmbH (DLR). It was an exceptionally clean and modern symbol, and survived a series of mergers that culminated in the foundation of Deutsche Luft Hansa AG. In the late 1960s, Lufthansa turned to the co-founder of the pioneering Hochschule für Gestaltung Ulm, Otl Aicher, to review its identity. Aicher adjusted the symbol – streamlining the bird, placing it within a circle and introducing the Helvetica Bold logotype – but it was the discipline with which the logo and Aicher's house style were applied that had a major influence on modern corporate identity. The designer laid down rules on colours, typefaces, grids and photographic style, and created systems for the design of packaging, advertising, exhibitions, uniforms and even interior furnishings. Aicher's principles set a template for all future large-scale identity programmes, including his own monumental project for the Munich Olympic Games.

13/AKDMKS Women
Fashion label, USA.
Designed by Matthias Ernstberger, 2004
A symbol for an 'urban denim' label by Akademiks, New York.

14/Nestlé
Packaged food and confectionery manufacturer, Switzerland. Designed by Henri Nestlé, 1868; modified by Nestlé, 1995
Henri Nestlé was a Swiss pharmacist who developed an alternative source of nutrition for babies who were intolerant of breast milk. He adopted his own family crest as the company logo; in his German dialect, 'Nestlé' means 'little nest'. The image of a mother bird

feeding her young could not be bettered. The only significant change in 140 years is that one of the three chicks in the original emblem has taken flight – a sign, perhaps, of falling birth rates in Nestlé's main markets. (Reproduced with the kind permission of Société des Produits Nestlé S.A.)

15/Crane & Co
Business paper manufacturer, USA. Designed by Chermayeff & Geismar Inc. (D: Steff Geissbuhler), 1987

16/Waterways Trust
Conservation and promotion of canals and rivers, UK. Designed by Pentagram (D: John Rushworth), 2000

Oakville Grocery
SINCE 1881

01/

02/

03/

04/

05/

06/

07/

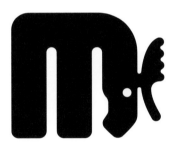

01/Oakville Grocery
California food stores, USA. Designed by Turner Duckworth (AD: David Turner, Bruce Duckworth), 2005

02/Taburet
Furniture retailer, Denmark. Designed by Designbolaget, 2004
A tabouret is a stool, hence the three-legged sheep.

03/Medima
Thermal underwear manufacturer, Germany. Designed 1956
Lampi, the Medima hare, stands for a business that makes thermal underwear from the fur of the Angora rabbit. He remains one of Germany's best-known trademarks.

04/Qantas
International airline, Australia. Designed by Lunn Design Group, 1984
The original kangaroo on Qantas (Queensland and Northern Territory Aerial Services) planes was adapted from the Australian one-penny coin. A winged kangaroo symbol, created by Sydney designer Gert Sellheim, was introduced in 1946 and lasted nearly 40 years, until the current non-flying marsupial was designed by Tony Lunn.

05/Kipling
Casual bag manufacturer, Belgium. Designed 1987
The founders of what was originally a high-quality backpack business wanted a name that was universally understood and free from unforeseen linguistic traps or pronunciation problems. They settled on Kipling, a name associated the world over with 'The Jungle Book', fun and adventure. The monkey followed and became a totem for the brand; every collection carries its own miniature monkey character.

06/The Antler
New York-German restaurant, USA. Designed by Sagmeister Inc (CD: Stefan Sagmeister; D: Matthias Ernstberger), 2004

07/Squirrel
Children's clothing manufacturer, UK. Designed by Unreal, 2005

08/Buffalo Pawn
Dallas pawn shop, USA. Designed by Marc English Design, 1994
A logo that combines the three circles of the Medici crest – the pawn symbol – with native American art and Wild West typography.

09/Libearty
Campaign for the protection of bears, UK. Designed by Spencer du Bois, 1992

10/Dodge
Vehicle manufacturer, USA. Designed 1981
First seen as a bonnet ornament in the early 1930s, the Dodge ram lasted into the 1960s. It made a return on trucks in the 1980s and then on all Dodge vehicles in 1996.

11/Minnesota Zoo
Zoo, USA. Designed by Lance Wyman, 1979
The Minnesota moose bows to make an 'M'.

2.33 Wildlife

13/

14/

15/

PLAYBOY

16/

12/WWF
Charitable conservation foundation, Switzerland
Designed by Sir Peter Scott, 1961; modified by
Landor Associates, 1986
A symbol for a charity has to be very special to
command the level of recognition of a heavily
marketed global brand. A potent, universally
appealing symbol can make up – in part, at least –
for a charity's limited visibility. The founders of WWF
knew exactly what they were doing back in 1961 to
win hearts. As co-founder Sir Peter Scott said at
the time: 'We wanted an animal that is beautiful, is
endangered, and one loved by people around the
world. We also wanted an animal that symbolised
all that was disappearing in the natural world.' The
image of a large furry panda looking up with big
black-patched eyes had practical benefits, too: it
transcended language barriers and carried impact
in inexpensively printed black-and-white campaign
literature. It was the widely covered arrival of the
giant panda Chi-Chi at London Zoo that was the
inspiration. Sketches by British environmentalist
Gerald Watterson were developed by Scott into
a finished symbol, whose legs were straightened
and whose ears and eyes were enlarged in 1986. In
2000, a MORI poll in the UK rated awareness of the
WWF logo at 77%.

13/San Francisco Zoo
Conservation zoo, USA.
Designed by Pentagram
(D: Kit Hinrichs), 2002

14/Nordisk Film
Producer and distributor
of films and electronic
games, Denmark.
Designed by Ole Olsen,
1906; updated 2006
Like Pathé's rooster, the
real polar bear atop
a globe that opened
Nordisk Film's earliest
productions acted as a
guarantor of quality and
integrity. The logo was
last updated to mark the
company's centenary.

15/Brand Australia
Tourism campaign,
Australia. Designed by
FutureBrand Melbourne,
2003

16/Playboy
Multimedia
entertainment company,
USA. Designed by Art
Paul, 1954
Paul was a freelance
designer in New York
when publisher Hugh
Hefner commissioned
him to create a symbol
for his new men's
magazine. 'The New
Yorker' and 'Esquire'
both used men as
their symbols, so Paul
went for wry innuendo:
a rabbit, chosen for
its humorous sexual
connotation and
dressed in a tuxedo to
add sophistication. He
did one drawing in half
an hour and sent it off
to Hefner. By issue 2,
the bunny was on the
front cover.

Bluewater
KENT

C☉ntinental

TAYMOUTH
SCOTLAND

PIAFFE
BEAUTY

ZEBRA HALL

04/   05/   06/

Black♞

07/

01/Bluewater
Retail centre, UK.
Designed by Minale
Tattersfield, 1999
When Bluewater was
designed, the owner,
Lend Lease, used a
system of imagery that
grounded the centre
in its location close to
the River Thames and
just inside the county
of Kent. Inside, carved
stone friezes recalled
London's historic guilds,
and maps in the stone
floors evoked the
maritime history of
the Thames. The logo
echoes the symbol
of Kent (a unicorn),
showing it at play in the
blue water of the lakes
that were originally
found in the abandoned
chalk pit where the
centre was built.

02/Continental
Manufacturer of tyres
and vehicle parts,
Germany. Designed 1876
Continental's first
prancing steed
was applied to the
company's horse-hoof
buffers, but quickly
became the trademark
for all of its rubber
products. Over the
following decades the
mark and the logotype
both developed and
eventually coalesced
into a single logo.
Continental was
founded in Hanover,
an area famous for its
horse-breeding, and
the coat of arms of the
Kingdom of Hanover
included a near-
identical animal.

03/Taymouth
Highland retreat, UK.
Designed by Glazer,
2005
Aiming to become
Europe's first seven-
star destination after
refurbishment, Taymouth
Castle in the Scottish
Highlands needed
an identity to attract
investors.

**04/Binghamton Visitor
Center**
Permanent tourism
exhibit, USA. Designed
by Chermayeff &
Geismar Inc. (D:
Emanuela Frigerio), 1998
Binghamton, in the
Susquehanna Heritage
Area of upstate New
York, is home to six
antique carousels –
the largest collection
in the world.

05/Piaffe Beauty
Cosmetics and skincare
brand, USA. Designed by
karlssonwilker, 2002
Piaffe is the name of a
movement performed by
horses – a balletic trot
on the spot – as part of
dressage.

06/Zebra Hall
Online toy retailer, USA.
Designed by Turner
Duckworth (AD:
David Turner, Bruce
Duckworth), 2003
'Fun and whimsical, yet
"Tiffany-esque"', was
the design brief for this
high-end toyshop's
identity.

07/Black Knight
Printer, UK. Designed by
Sam Dallyn, 2004

2.35 Cats and
dogs

01/

02/

03/

04/

05/

06/

07/

  **FASHION LAB.**

08/ 09/ 10/

11/

01/Red Lion Court
Barristers' chambers, UK. Designed by Johnson Banks, 1994–95
Chambers of the London legal world are customarily named after their address. In this case, a lion drawn in red legal ribbon says it all.

02/Mascot
Dog accessories retailer, USA. Designed by Bob Dinetz Design, 2005
The logo honours the Mascot owner's beloved Boston Terrier.

03/Alvarez Gomez
Perfumier, Spain. Designed by Pentagram (D: Fernando Gutierrez), 2006
An identity that retains the old-fashioned charm of this Madrid perfumería, whose own fragrances, based on long-forgotten recipes, are back in fashion.

04/Jaguar
Performance car manufacturer, UK. Designed by The Partners (AD: Greg Quinton; D: Steve Owen, Helen Cooley), 2002
A new identity for Jaguar supported the launch of new models and followed a decade of engineering and vehicle design initiatives put in place by Ford, the company's owner since 1992. The leaping jaguar was digitally remodelled to create a more dynamic but crafted symbol, and its logotype was updated.

05/DoveLewis
Emergency animal hospital, USA. Designed by Sandstrom Design, 2005

06/Gartmore
Financial services, UK. Designed by Corporate Edge, 2002

07/Cunard Line
Cruise line, UK. Designed by Siegel & Gale, 1997
Cunard's association with a lion rampant is probably the result of its close relationship with the East India Company in the mid-19th century, whose crest bore a similar symbol. A globe was added to indicate Cunard's routes across the Atlantic, and a crown to denote its foundation under government contract (as a transatlantic mail carrier). Founder Samuel Cunard was frequently referred to as the 'Steam Lion'.

08/Savana
Paint and dye manufacturer, Romania. Designed by Brandient, 2005
Making a connection with wild animals and colour, this identity has revitalized a paint brand that was starting to look dried up.

09/JVP (Jerusalem Venture Partners)
Venture Capital Fund, Israel. Designed by Chermayeff & Geismar Inc. (D: Steff Geissbuhler, Melanie Kirchner), 2004

10/Fashion Lab.
Fashion retailer, The Netherlands. Designed by ankerxstrijbos, 2006
'Lab' for 'Labrador', rather than laboratory, after the owner's ever-present in this small store for contemporary Scandinavian fashion. The dog's red ball provides the full stop.

11/Festival Nouveau Cinéma
Film and new media festival, Canada. Designed 2002

02/ ....

03/ ....

04/ ....

05/ ....

06/ ....

07/ ....

01/Starbucks
Coffee house chain, USA
Designed by Heckler Associates, 1987; modified by Heckler Associates, 1992
Starbucks Coffee, Tea and Spice was founded in Seattle in 1971 with a brown circular logo containing a 16th-century Norse woodcut of a bare-breasted two-tailed mermaid, or siren. Only when it was sold to Howard Schultz, the owner of espresso café chain Il Giornale, did the brand take off. The mermaid was placed in a green circle (inherited from the logo for Il Giornale) and redrawn, and the name was shortened to Starbucks Coffee. In 1992, Terry Heckler revisited the logo and focused on the top half of the smiling siren.

02/Meoclinic
Private medical clinic, Germany. Designed by Thomas Manss & Company, 1998
The functionalism of traditional healthcare branding is shunned in the identity for this luxury clinic. The symbolism of the calligraphic phoenix – rejuvenation and purity – is understood by the clinic's international clientele.

03/Godiva Chocolatier
Premium confectioner, Belgium. Designed by Pentagram (D: Michael Bierut), 1993
What associations Brussels confectioner Joseph Draps was making when he chose Godiva as the name for

his chocolate and shop are not clear. Godiva was the comely wife of Leofric the Dane, and her naked ride through the city of Coventry spared its citizens her husband's heavy taxes – as long as they didn't sneak a peek.

04/Superior Scientific
Biomedical instruments, USA. Designed by HLC Group Inc (D: Hoi L Chu), 1983
A serpent spells out the company's initials on an oscilloscope. The snake's association with medicine began with the Rod of Asclepius, an ancient Greek symbol named after a surgeon who was thought to have brought patients back from the dead.

05/The Loch Ness Partnership
Visitor attraction development group, UK. Designed by Navyblue Design Group (D: Nick Needham), 2005

06/Janus Capital Group
Mutual fund manager, USA. Designed by Templin Brink Design (CD: Joel Templin, Gaby Brink), 2003
Although often seen today as a symbol of hypocrisy, Janus is also the Roman god of beginnings and endings and has the ability to look both backwards and forwards – a desirable asset for a fund manager.

07/Goodyear
Tyres and vehicle parts, USA. Designed 1900
Goodyear's winged foot has its origins in the Akron family home of Frank Seiberling, the company founder. On a post on the stairway stood a statue of Mercury, the Roman god of trade and commerce, which, Seiberling suggested, embodied the attributes that Goodyear products were known for: speed and safe carriage.

01/

02/

03/

04/

05/

06/

07/

08/

09/

10/

11/

01/KidStart
Loyalty scheme, UK.
Designed by 300million
(D: Martin Lawless), 2005
Consumers can
contribute to their
child's trust fund by
making purchases from
the scheme's retail
members.

**02/Counterpunch
Trading**
Online training for
investment traders,
USA. Designed by
Design Ranch (AD:
Michelle Sonderegger,
Ingred Sidie; D: Michelle
Martynowicz, Tad
Carpenter), 2004
Like boxing, trading
investments is about
picking your moment.

**03/Alvin Ailey American
Dance Theater**
Contemporary dance
company, USA.
Designed by Chermayeff
& Geismar Inc. (D: Steff
Geissbuhler), 1981

04/Michelin
Tyre manufacturer,
France. Designed
by O'Galop (Marius
Rossillon), 1898
A pile of tyres on the
company's stand at
Lyon Universal Exhibition
of 1894 caught the eye
of Edward Michelin. He
turned to his brother:
'Look, with arms, it
would make a man.'
André remembered the
remark a few years later
when he saw a poster
for a brasserie with a
bearded giant raising
a glass. He asked the

artist O'Galop to replace
the giant with a man
made of tyres holding
a cup full of nails and
glass, proclaiming,
'Cheers, the Michelin
tyre toasts obstacles!'
The poster was titled
after the Latin quotation
by Horace: 'Nunc est
bibendum' ('Now is the
time to drink'). Monsieur
Bibendum has since
lost some pounds
and his cigar, but has
gained familiarity and
cartoonish joie de vivre.

05/Vrijwilligerspas
Discount card for
cultural events, to
promote volunteering,
The Netherlands.
Designed by Studio
Bau Winkel, 2000

**06/Durham School
Services**
School transportation
services, USA. Designed
by Pentagram (D: Lowell
Williams), 2002
Durham serves more
than 300 school districts
throughout the USA.

07/Ronnie Teape
Pianist and music
teacher, UK. Designed
by Roundel (D: John
Bateson, Adam Browne),
2005

08/Tony Awards
American Theatre Wing's
annual awards, USA.
Designed by Siegel &
Gale, 2006
Capturing the emotion of
the awards ceremony,
the logo forms part of
an identity that uses
silhouettes of famous
Broadway performances
on items like stationery
and billboards.

**09/National Basketball
Association**
Basketball league, USA.
Designed by Siegel &
Gale, 1970
A breakthrough for
the design company's
founder Alan Siegel
came when he based
the NBA logo on a photo
of Hall-of-Famer Jerry
West and created an
American sports icon.

10/Toi Com Moi
Online fashion retailer,
France. Designed
by FL@33 (D: Agathe
Jacquillat, Tomi
Vollauschek), 2003
Toi Com Moi ('you like
me') is a Paris-based
retailer of matching
clothes for parents and
children.

11/Karl Lagerfeld
Luxury women's fashion
label, USA. Designed by
Boy Bastiaens, 2006
Created as part of the
repositioning of the Karl
Lagerfeld brand by new
owner, Tommy Hilfiger.

01/

SINCE 1870

SAN FRANCISCO
LAW LIBRARY

02/   03/   04/

05/

01/Taíi
Financial services, Brazil. Designed by FutureBrand BC&H, 2005
Offering financial services for customers on low incomes, Taíi is part of Banco Itaú.

02/San Francisco Law Library
Public legal library, USA. Designed by Templin Brink Design (CD: Joel Templin, Gaby Brink; D: Brian Gunderson), 2005

03/Knucklehead
Film and commercial directors, UK. Designed by Johnson Banks, 2004–05

04/Survival International
Charity, UK. Designed by Spencer du Bois (D: John Spencer), 1990
SI helps to preserve the traditional ways of life of tribal people around the world.

05/Everyclick.com
Charitable search engine, UK.
Designed by Arthur-SteenHorneAdamson, 2005
This mark for a search engine had to be instantly recognizable in any context, classless, nationless and yet engender a sense of community. Everyclick donates 50% of its revenue to charity. Every click counts.

06/United Way of America
Community-based charity, USA. Designed by Saul Bass and Mamoru Shimokochi, 1973; modified by FutureBrand, 2004
A network of approximately 1300 locally governed organizations in the USA and 44 other countries, United Way commissioned Saul Bass to create a symbol that would bring harmony to the way each chapter presented itself. Thirty years later, history was repeating itself; only 11% of chapters were using an approved version of the 'helping hand' logo. When the organization introduced measures to increase

the accountability and performance of chapters, FutureBrand was brought in to reflect the change and to 'correct technical flaws' in the previous logo.

07/Minnesota Children's Museum
Children's museum, USA. Designed by Pentagram (D: Michael Bierut), 1995
Photographs of children's hands are used throughout the identity system and were inspired by the 'hands-on' exhibits and activities throughout the museum.

08/Yellow
Business directory, Australia. Designed by FutureBrand Melbourne
Now available online and on mobile phones, Australia's Yellow Pages business directory rebranded without the 'Pages'. The walking fingers are now clicking, too.

09/Truce International
Peace campaign, UK. Designed by Pentagram (D: Fernando Gutierrez), 2004
Truce 'aims to use strategic partnerships for peace' and was established under the patronage of then England football manager Sven-Göran Eriksson and his partner, Nancy Dell'Olio. The

logo's inspiration came from the legendary World War I kick-about between German and British soldiers on Boxing Day 1914.

11/

12/

13/

NATIONAL
**CAMPAIGN
AGAINST YOUTH
VIOLENCE**

14/

10/Secours Populaire Français
Non-profit humanitarian association, France
Designed by Grapus, 1981
'In order to touch the viewer, an image has to go through the filter of your personal experience and inner convictions.' This quote from Pierre Bernard (http://www.aigany.org/ideas/features/bernard) explains the French designer's personal, often very raw approach to design; it does not encompass the political commitment that drove him and his co-designers in the legendary Grapus collective to produce some of the most powerful graphic propaganda of the 1970s. Grapus was founded by Bernard and two other members of the PCF (French Communist Party) in the wake of the 1968 student rebellions in Paris. They rejected commercial clients and designed posters and symbols for local authorities, charities and trade unions. Their colourful, undisciplined and often naïve designs were in direct opposition to conventional corporate design, and inspired students the world over. But after François Mitterrand's Socialist government came to power in 1981, design for public bodies and social groups went mainstream, leaving Grapus in an ideological limbo. The group disbanded in 1991, leaving a design legacy unique in its vitality, intensity and passion.

11/GOAT Food and Beverage Co
Nutritious food company, USA.
Designed by Arnell Group, 2006
A line of nutritious snacks and drinks, GOAT is produced by Mars and is the brainchild of Muhammad Ali (Greatest Of All Time = GOAT) and brand consultant Peter Arnell, who lost 250lb through healthy eating.

12/Caffè Leggero
Café chain, Japan.
Designed by Bravis International, 2005
The same company that owns Japan's MOS Burger restaurants developed this chain of European-style cafés. Its identity aims for a laid-back Europe-meets-Manhattan sophistication.

13/Seresin Estates
Vineyard, New Zealand.
Designed by CDT, 1997
Everything at Seresin Estates, including the harvesting of grapes, is done by hand, an ethos reflected by the use of owner Michael Seresin's handprint in the identity.

14/ National Campaign Against Youth Violence
Programme to combat youth violence, USA.
Designed by Templin Brink Design (CD: Joel Templin, Gaby Brink; D: Felix Sockwell), 2000
The NCAYV was initiated by Bill Clinton during his last year as president to address the epidemic rates of youth violence in the USA.

01/

02/

03/

ROYAL ARMOURIES MUSEUM

BRAINSHELL

01/Girl Scouts of the USA
Youth organization for girls, USA. Designed by Saul Bass, 1978; modified by Siegel & Gale, 1999

02/Mutual of Omaha
Financial services, USA. Designed by Crosby Associates, 2001
The logo features a chief of the Sioux tribe, which once occupied the land that became Omaha, Nebraska.

03/Wella
Haircare products, Germany. Designed by Claus Koch Corporate Communications, 1993
Long, streaming tresses have represented Wella since 1927, but up until 1993 the head appeared as a solid colour. The redesign endowed the hair with a more natural wave and the head with a more feminine profile.

04/Royal Armouries Museum
Museum of arms and armour, UK. Designed by Minale Tattersfield, 1996
The identity for this Leeds museum, which was created to showcase artefacts that had been hidden for years in the Tower of London archives, shows a war mask/helmet worn by Henry VIII. Known as a Ram's Head, this piece of royal armoury was an apt choice for the RAM.

05/Brainshell
Patent exploitation agency, Germany. Designed by Thomas Manss & Company, 2003
Brainshell markets the patent rights of scientists' inventions at Brandenburg's eight universities and colleges: an interface between academia and business, technology and the marketplace.

look-look

01/

02/

03/

Community
Preparatory
School

04/

05/

06/

07/

01/Look-Look
Youth market research
and trend-forecasting
agency, USA. Designed
by Open, 1999

02/Ossip Optometry
Private eye care
practices, USA.
Designed by Lodge
Design (D: Eric Kass),
2002
Dr Kenneth Ossip
opened his optometry
practice in Broad Ripple,
Indianapolis, in 1952.
The company now
has nine practices
across Indiana.

03/Sign Design Society
Trade body for
practitioners of signing
and wayfinding, UK.
Designed by Atelier
Works, 1991
A sign is not a sign if it
isn't seen. This logo is
composed of a sign and
the eye that sees it.

04/Shopping.com
Comparison shopping
website, USA. Designed
by Turner Duckworth
(AD: David Turner, Bruce
Duckworth), 2003
A potentially dry
technical product
is given an inviting
personality by
combining the positive
symbol of a tick box
with a shopping bag to
conjure a smiling face.

**05/Community
Preparatory School**
Middle school, USA.
Designed by Malcolm
Grear Designers, 1989
Community Prep
offers educational
opportunities to children
from low-income
families in the area
of Providence,
Rhode Island.

**06/Private Sector
Development**
World Bank online
'knowledge hub', USA.
Designed by Peter
Grundy, 2000
With the aim of
stimulating business
and employment
opportunities for the
poor in developing
countries, this division of
the World Bank provides
data and information on
financial and private-
sector development.

07/Innocent
Natural fruit drink
manufacturer, UK.
Designed by Deepend,
1999
A saintly but fruity
logo, playful writing
and, above all,
unadulterated drinks
have made Innocent
one of the UK's fastest
growing companies.

2.40 Eyes and
faces

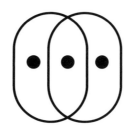

09/

10/

11/

12/

08/TimeWarner Cable
Cable TV group, USA
Designed by Chermayeff & Geismar Inc. (D: Steff Geissbuhler), 1990
In the USA it is impossible to escape the work of Ivan Chermayeff and Tom Geismar. Since opening their first studio with Robert Brownjohn in 1957, the pair and their successive companies have rebranded leading American organizations in every field of business, including NBC, Xerox and Mobil, and created some of the smartest, most concise and enduring identities of the last 50 years. For 30 of those years, Swiss designer Steff Geissbuhler was a key part of Chermayeff & Geismar's success. The identity for TimeWarner Cable was originally for the parent group, which was formed when Time Inc and Warner Communications merged in 1990. Their combined strengths, journalism and entertainment, demanded a visual common denominator, and Geissbuhler's eye-ear pictograph symbolized the union as a natural fit. In 2005, Chermayeff & Geismar Inc. was dissolved following the departure of Geissbuhler and several senior colleagues, who established their own successful firm, C&G Partners. Chermayeff and Geismar, meanwhile, continue to design for major clients as Chermayeff & Geismar Studio.

09/Andrews McMeel Universal
Publishing and press syndicate group, USA. Designed by Chermayeff & Geismar Inc. (D: Steff Geissbuhler), 1995
Founded as Universal Press Syndicate, Andrews McMeel Universal diversified. Its mark makes use of the one consistent initial in both names and adds a pair of eyes for reading.

10/Eye To Eye
Cultural relations conference, UK. Designed by Atelier Works, 2002

11/Carol Delong
Performance artist, USA. Designed by Crosby Associates, 1982

12/LG
Industrial conglomerate, South Korea. Designed 1995
Created as Lucky-Goldstar in 1947, this South Korean chaebol, known mainly for its consumer electronics, abbreviated its name in 1995. In common with many Far Eastern businesses, LG has an explanation for every element of its corporate symbol. It is not sufficient to claim, as it does, that the symbol 'represents the world, future, youth, humanity and technology'. The presence of a single eye, says LG, shows the brand to be 'goal-oriented, focused, confident', while the upper-right-hand space is 'left blank and asymmetric, which represents LG's creativity and adaptability to change'.

01/

02/

03/

Land
Heritage

01/BabyBoom Records
Record label, UK.
Designed by Funnel
Creative, 2006
The label's initials, BBR,
are transformed into
three hearts to convey
the founders' strength
of feeling for music and
for the discovery of
new talent.

02/Heart
Local radio station
franchise, UK. Designed
by BB/Saunders, 2004
Vying for top spot in
London with Capital and
Magic, Heart is the key
station in the Chrysalis
radio portfolio. The
rebrand in 2004 created
a more contemporary
image.

**03/New York City
Health and Hospitals
Corporation**
Municipal hospitals and
healthcare system, USA.
Designed by Chermayeff
& Geismar Inc. (D: Steff
Geissbuhler), 1988

04/Land Heritage
Organic farming
charity, UK. Designed
by Together Design
(D: Heidi Lightfoot, Katja
Thielen, Martin Lawless,
Mike Pratley)
Needing to raise funds
for a model farm project,
Land Heritage turned
to Together Design
to devise an identity
that would raise the
charity's profile. The
symbol strikes a balance
between conveying
professionalism and a
love of the land.

05/Heartbrand
Umbrella ice cream
brand, UK. Designed by
Carter Wong Tomlin, 1996
Unilever is the world's
biggest manufacturer of
ice cream, with over £3
billion in annual sales.
Having accumulated
more than 50 brands
around the world,
including Wall's in
the UK and Algida in
southern Europe, the
company took the step
of harmonizing them all
under one identity to
increase international
brand awareness and
to create economies of
scale in packaging and
storage. Heartbrand
was recently voted one
of the top-ten most
recognizable brands
worldwide.

06/

**Lenox Hill
Heart and Vascular
Institute
of New York**

PENSION
H⊙E⊛R⊙Z

MOSS
PHARMACY

07/   08/   09/

10/

sundhed.dk

11/ 12/ 13/

14/

06/A2 Type Foundry
Graphic design studio
type library, UK.
Designed by A2/SW/HK,
2005

07/Lenox Hill Heart and Vascular Institute of New York
Cardio-vascular care
programme, USA.
Designed by Arnold Saks
Associates, 1998
An identity for one of the
USA's leading treatment
centres for conditions
affecting the heart and
arteries.

08/Pension Herz
Hyogo Prefecture guest
house, Japan. Designed
by Katsuichi Ito Design
Studio, 1996

09/Moss Pharmacy
National pharmacy
chain, UK. Designed
by Glazer, 1999
Pharmaceuticals,
the chemist's green
cross and two hearts,
indicating a warmth not
usually associated with
pharmacists, combine in
this logo for a chain with
over 600 outlets.

10/Felt
Charities' fundraising
campaign, UK. Designed
by Funnel Creative, 2005
Felt is a campaign by
four charities in the
north west of England to
encourage more people
to leave legacies to
charities. A flower is
formed from a quartet
of hearts.

11/Crêpe Affaire
French pancake
restaurant chain, UK.
Designed by Mind
Design, 2005
Crêpe Affaire was
launched as a dating
spot for crêpe lovers,
hence the circumflex's
transformation.

12/Claddagh
Irish pub chain, USA.
Designed by Lodge
Design (D: Eric Kass),
2003
Lodge Design
specializes in 'retro'
identities that recall
graphic styles of
yesteryear. This
pastiche of vintage beer
labels is the logo for
what is now a chain of
Irish-themed pubs and
restaurants across the
Midwest. As well as this
clean version there is
an artificially weathered
option for added
authenticity.

13/Sundhed.dk
Online public health
portal, Denmark
Designed by Bysted,
2002

14/The Art Fund
Membership
organization, UK.
Designed by Johnson
Banks, 2006
Donations from members
of The Art Fund help
UK galleries keep art in
the country. Although it
looks natural, the union
of a heart and a frame,
expressing members'
love of art, took a while
to make fit.

THE
ROYAL
PARKS

02/

03/

04/

05/

06/

07/

01/The Royal Parks
Parks maintenance and conservation agency, UK
Designed by Moon Communications (D: Richard Moon, Ceri Webber, Andy Locke), 1996
The Royal Parks, the agency maintaining such spaces as Hyde Park, Green Park and Greenwich Park in London, needed an identity. According to protocol, tenders (including initial concepts) from 10 companies had to be opened at the same moment in one room at the client's offices. An uneasy silence descended; the design that stood out – a crown made of leaves from the parks' trees – went directly against the requirement that no liberties were to be taken with the Royal Coats of Arms. Nevertheless, the design was sent to Buckingham Palace in 1992, along with the second and third choices as an insurance policy. A wait of three to seven months for a reply would have been usual. Within 24 hours Her Majesty had approved the identity.

02/Husqvarna
Manufacturer of forestry and garden products and power cutters, Sweden. Designed 1972
Husqvarna was founded as a rifle factory in 1689, and its symbol started life as a hand-etched hallmark of a passed musket, with three ridges indicating the sight on the gun barrel. When the business diversified in the early 20th century, the logo morphed into an ornate crest topped by a crown. A more functional version appeared in 1972.

03/Crown
Entertainment complex, Australia. Designed by FutureBrand Melbourne, 1998
An identity intended to pull in the high rollers to this gaming, hotel, retail, restaurant and entertainment complex in Melbourne.

04/PET
State security intelligence service, Denmark. Designed by Kontrapunkt, 2003
Partially shrouded in secrecy, like the work of PET.

05/gsus
Fashion label, The Netherlands. Designed by Jan Schrijver, 1993
Striking a fashionably blasphemous note, the crown of thorns was drawn by the streetwear label's co-founder.

06/National Museet
Museum of national culture, Denmark. Designed by Kontrapunkt, 1992

07/Fürst Thurn und Taxis
Trust management, Germany. Designed by Büro für Gestaltung Wangler & Abele, 2004
The princely house of Thurn und Taxis ('fürst' is German for 'prince') resides at St Emmeram Castle in Regensburg and is one of the wealthiest families in Germany. This logo identifies the administration of the family trust.

NEW LEAF
PAPER

01/

TIME WARNER
BOOKS

02/

Reid_Me

03/

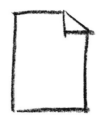

04/

05/

BLACKFORDS

06/

AWARDS for NATIONAL
NEWSPAPER ADVERTISING

07/

MAD Moose Press

THE
SCOTSMAN
EDINBURGH

08/   09/   10/

PocketCard

11/

01/New Leaf Paper
Environmentally
responsible paper
manufacturer, USA.
Designed by Elixir
Design, 1999

02/Time Warner Books
Publishing imprint, USA.
Designed by Unreal,
2005

03/Peter Reid
Copywriter, UK.
Designed by The
Partners (AD: Nina
Jenkins; D: Bob Young,
Sophie Hayes, Rob
Holloway), 2005
The icon for a new
word-processing
document is a
familiar sight for any
professional writer.

04/Good Paper
Paper brand, USA.
Designed by BBK Studio,
1999
Claiming that its paper
is high performance and
all-purpose, this brand
must be a godsend
to designers.

**05/Volunteer Reading
Help**
National charity for
children with reading
difficulties, UK. Designed
by Spencer du Bois (D:
John Spencer), 1997
The experience of
reading with a child
is instantly evoked by
the two hands of this
symbol.

06/Blackfords
Litho printer, UK.
Designed by Glazer
A turning of the page
spells out the initial
of this family-run litho
printing company.

**07/Awards for National
Newspaper Advertising**
Creative award scheme,
UK. Designed by
SomeOne (D: David Law,
Laura Hussey, Simon
Manchipp), 2004

08/Mad Moose Press
Publisher, UK. Designed
by Saatchi Design, 2000

09/The Scotsman Hotel
Luxury hotel, UK.
Designed by SomeOne,
2005
This Edinburgh hotel
is named after the
previous occupant of
its noble premises: 'The
Scotsman' newspaper.
To recall that history
and to provide opening
conversational gambits
with guests, a
newspaper icon was
chosen for the hotel's
identity, enlivened by
a digitized version of a
bespoke Elgin tweed.

10/CMP
Paper distributor, USA.
Designed by BBK Studio,
2005
Smart paper, fast, is the
message from this logo.

11/PocketCard
Payment system, USA.
Designed by Segura
Inc, 2003
PocketCard is an
electronic payment
service that provides
supervised access to
funds for teenagers,
students, family
members and expense-
account employees.

PREMIER RUGBY

01/

International Cricket Council

A-LEAGUE

02/

03/

04/

05/

06/   07/   08/

09/

01/Premier Rugby
Rugby union super
league, UK. Designed
by Glazer
The identity for
the organization
representing the UK's
12 elite rugby union
clubs reflects the
strength and fluidity of
the game at its best.

**02/International Cricket
Council**
World governing body
for cricket, United Arab
Emirates. Designed by
Minale Tattersfield, 2001

03/Payless Shoes TWisM
Athletic shoes brand,
USA. Designed by
Design Ranch (AD:
Michelle Sonderegger,
Ingred Sidie; D: Michelle
Martynowicz, Tad
Carpenter), 2005
An identity for a shoe
brand endorsed by
former basketball star
Shaquille O'Neal under
the name of his motto:
TWisM – 'The World
is Mine'.

04/A-League
Premier football league,
Australia. Designed by
Coast Design (Sydney),
2004
Eight 'A' shapes
wrapped around a ball
represent the league's
eight clubs.

05/Domo
Home appliance
retailer, Romania.
Designed by Brandient,
2005
Toy balls associate
this white goods retail
chain with family life,
and back up its claim to
be 'the home of home
appliances'.

06/TennisBC
Sports association,
Canada. Designed by
Subplot Design (CD:
Matthew Clark, Roy
White), 2006
A fast-growing
provincial sports
organization promoting
tennis in British
Columbia, TennisBC
needed a new identity
to reflect its increase in
stature and to attract
new corporate sponsors.

The mark makes the
letters 'BC' from the lines
on a tennis ball.

07/RoboCup Osaka
Robot football
tournament, Japan.
Designed by
kokokumaru (D:
Yoshimaru Takahashi),
2005
RoboCup is an
international initiative
that fosters robotic
research by setting a
standard challenge – a
football tournament – at
which the latest robots
can be tested.

08/The Modern Ball
Biennial fundraising
gala, USA. Designed by
Elixir Design, 2004
The non-profit San
Francisco Museum of
Modern Art instituted
a biennial gala in
2004 to raise funds
for exhibitions and
education projects.
Its identity is flexible
enough to be refreshed
for each future ball.

09/British Golf Museum
Sporting museum, UK.
Designed by Tayburn,
2004
By balancing a sense of
heritage with a feeling
for the excitement of the
modern game, the new
brand, launched during
the 250th anniversary
year of the Royal and
Ancient Golf Club of
St Andrews, seeks to
attract visitors of
all ages.

01/

02/

03/

04/

05/

06/

07/

01/Creative Byline
Online writing agency,
USA. Designed by BBK
Studio, 2006
Creative Byline helps
to attract publishers
to undiscovered
authors (with magnetic
manuscripts).

**02/Cleanskin Clearing
House**
Wine retailer, Australia.
Designed by Parallax,
2002
CCH specializes in
cleanskin, or unlabelled,
wine; its logo depicts the
entrance to an exclusive
source of bargains for
wine lovers.

03/City of Leiden
Local authority, The
Netherlands. Designed
by Eden, 1993
Leiden, an historic
city in the north of the
country, wanted to
present itself as an
accessible citizen-
oriented community.
The keys from its coat of
arms had to be retained,
so Eden combined
them with a door that is
always open.

04/Cliff Hanger
Mountain clothing
retailer, UK. Designed
by DA Design (D: David
Azurdia), 2006

05/Rar Lyd
Record label,
Denmark. Designed by
Designbolaget, 2004
Rar Lyd – 'feel-good
sounds' – represents
folk musicians and
singer-songwriters.
It targets people 'who
don't like modern music',
and who might, as a
consequence, carry
a pair of earplugs in
their pocket.

**06/The Guild of Food
Writers**
Professional association
of food writers, UK.
Designed by 300million
(CD: Matt Baxter,
Martin Lawless;
D: Katie Morgan, Natalie
Bennett), 2005
The pen is mightier
than the pudding, but
they co-exist more than
happily in this award-
winning identity.

07/Made To Play
Record label, UK.
Designed by Malone
Design (D: David
Malone), 2005
Visual references
courtesy of Fisher Price.

08/Lincoln Stationers
Stationery retailer, USA.
Designed by Lance
Wyman, 1994
The identity for a New
York stationer across
the street from the
Lincoln Center for the
Performing Arts shows a
nib with the inscription
'LS', or is it a treble clef?

**09/My Cuisine Canary
Wharf**
Food delivery service,
UK. Designed by
Radford Wallis
(CD, D: Stuart Radford,
Andrew Wallis; D: Tim
Fellowes), 2006

**10/Watch City Brewing
Co**
Massachusetts micro-
brewery and restaurant,
USA. Designed by
Pentagram (D: Woody
Pirtle), 2001

11/Wordstock
Annual literature
festival, USA. Designed
by Bob Dinetz Design,
2005
A logo for a literature
festival in Portland,
Oregon, noted for its
level of intimacy with
authors.

2.45 Everyday
objects

12/

13/

14/

15/

16/

17/

18/

12/Lee Mallett
Urban regeneration consultancy, UK. Designed by Brownjohn (D: James Beveridge, Andy Mosley), 2005

13/Footstep Films
Travel guide film production company, UK. Designed by Purpose, 2004

14/Betty Crocker
Baking products brand, USA. Designed by Lippincott Mercer, 1950s

15/American Institute of Architects Center
Fundraising campaign for a new HQ, USA. Designed by Pentagram (D: Michael Gericke), 2001

16/Key Coffee
Coffee manufacturer, Japan. Designed by HLC Group (D: Hoi L Chu, Marco Ganz), 1989 Established in 1920, Kimura Coffee Company pioneered the development of the Japanese coffee industry with its 'Key' brand ('key' is an anglicization of 'Kimura'). Its 1989 redesign re-drew the traditional key and integrated it into the 'K'.

17/Under The Table Productions
Theatre production company, Australia. Designed by Saatchi Design, 2005

18/Israel Smith Photographers
Wedding and portrait photographer, Australia. Designed by Coast Design (Sydney), 2006 Elements from the photographer's life and beachside lifestyle create an appropriate light for a formal occasion.

19/SitOnIt Seating
Seating manufacturer, USA. Designed by BBK Studio, 2004 A chair-cum-open-box stands for a business that not only makes chairs but also delivers them quickly.

20/UK Music Week
Initiative to promote British music, UK. Designed by Together Design UK Music Week is a commercial radio initiative to promote British music of all genres through programming and events.

21/Matelsom
Mattress and bed manufacturer, France. Designed by FL@33 (D: Agathe Jacquillat, Tomi Vollauschek), 2002

22/Sister Ray Enterprises
Artist management company, USA. Designed by Sagmeister Inc (CD: Stefan Sagmeister; D: Matthias Ernstberger), 2002 Lou Reed's management company takes its name from the dissonant anthem he wrote for The Velvet Underground in 1967, while its logo features his trademark sunglasses.

ORANGE PEKOE

24/

25/

26/

27/

23/UBS
Financial services, Switzerland
Designed by Warja Lavater, 1937; updated by
Interbrand, 1998
Bank symbols tend to fall into two camps: strong
interlocking abstract forms aimed at engendering
a sense of security and stability; and stirring images
of animals – horses or lions – that are often seen as
more trustworthy than your average human.
But what could be a better symbol for a bank than
a set of keys? The UBS mark was originally created
for the Swiss Bank Corporation in 1937 by a Swiss
illustrator, Warja Lavater, fresh out of Zürich's
School of Applied Arts. With an eye on expansion
beyond Switzerland, the bank needed a symbol
with universal relevance. Lavater drew not one
but three keys, crossed to represent 'confidence,
security and discretion', as well as the country's
three linguistic communities. In 1998, when Swiss
Bank merged with the Union Bank of Switzerland,
a new logo combined the visual heritage of both
institutions. Lavater's keys were simplified only
slightly. Safe technology and banking generally
may have moved on but, in the age of Internet
fraud and identity theft, nothing evokes a sense
of security like a set of keys.

24/Walgreens
Drugstore chain, USA.
Designed 2006
Following a two-year
study into how to
update its image,
Walgreens dropped its
blue pestle-and-mortar
neon signs in favour
of a red version with
a scripted 'W' on the
side, which, it claims,
makes stores more
visible from a distance.
'I've envied McDonald's
for years with their
Golden Arches,' said
chairman and CEO David
Bernauer following the
announcement of
the change.

25/Orange Pekoe
Specialist tea room and
shop, UK. Designed
by Together Design
(D: Heidi Lightfoot,
Katja Thielen, Sabine
Schäfer), 2006

26/Imperial Laundry
Business premises, UK.
Designed by Unreal,
2005
A former Victorian
laundry in Battersea,
south London, the
Imperial Laundry has
been refurbished to
become a centre for
small interior design
and crafts companies.

**27/International Guitar
Foundation & Festivals**
Guitar courses,
workshops and
concerts, UK. Designed
by Mytton Williams
(D: Bob Mytton), 2001

BRIAN S NOLAN

Ireland's Home of Furnishings

01/

02/

03/

sesame
workshop™

DEUTSCHE
KINEMATHEK
MUSEUM
FÜR FILM UND
FERNSEHEN

01/Brian S Nolan
Furniture retailer, Ireland. Designed by Coast Design (Sydney), 2004
An identity for a long-established family-run furniture business that has its home in a heritage building in Dun Laoghaire, County Dublin.

02/Coram Family
Children's charity, UK. Designed by Pentagram (D: John McConnell), 2000
Thought to be England's oldest children's charity, Coram Family promotes best practice in the care of vulnerable children, especially in difficult areas. Its heritage extends back to the work of Captain Thomas Coram, who established the Foundling Hospital in 1739 to care for children abandoned on the streets of London.

03/ERA Real Estate
Residential property agency franchise, USA. Designed by Chermayeff & Geismar Inc. (D: Steff Geissbuhler), 1998
Electronic Realty Associates opened in 1972 with a mission to give homebuyers a better service through greater use of technology. Early adoption of the fax machine and, later, the Internet to help people buy and sell homes anywhere in the USA led to rapid growth. ERA now has operations in 28 countries.

04/Sesame Workshop
Non-profit children's TV production company, USA. Designed by Carbone Smolan Agency
Formerly the Children's Television Workshop, this production company underwent an identity change that capitalized on the awareness of its best-known production – 'Sesame Street' – to strengthen the brand's presence across media and its 200 licensees.

05/Verella Jeans
Denim fashion brand, USA. Designed by karlssonwilker (AD, D: Hjalti Karlsson, Jan Wilker), 2003

06/Integrated Living Communities
National chain of assisted-living communities, USA. Designed by Chermayeff & Geismar Inc. (D: Emanuela Frigerio), 1997

07/Deutsche Kinemathek – Museum für Film und Fernsehen
Film and television museum, Germany. Designed by Pentagram (D: Justus Oehler, Josephine Rank), 2006
Two overlapping screens – one for film, one for TV – make an 'M' and a home for the museum.

01/

02/

03/

04/

05/

LANDS'⋮END

NORTH ⋮ ABBEY

06/ ....

07/ ....

08/ ....

09/ ....

01/Conflict
Design store, The
Netherlands. Designed
by Boy Bastiaens, 2005
Conflict's name and
symbol of a castle
wreathed in dark
clouds follow the
store's philosophy of
creating 'uneasiness
in residence'.

**02/New York Botanical
Garden**
Botanical museum and
gardens, USA. Designed
by Pentagram (D: Paula
Scher), 2000
The 250-acre gardens
include a remnant of the
forest that once covered
Manhattan, but the
principal icon is the Enid
A Haupt Conservatory,
the largest Victorian
glasshouse in America.

**03/JF Willumsens
Museum**
Museum, Denmark.
Designed by e-types
The identity for this
museum devoted to
one artist features a
profile of Willumsen's
monumental twin
Art Deco sculptures,
'Ravnene', which stand
at the entrance to the
museum.

04/Galleria Colonna
Shopping and business
centre, Italy. Designed
by Pentagram (D: John
McConnell), 1990
Taking the place of the
initial 'C', a classical
column identifies this
refined shopping mall
in one of Rome's
historic arcades.

**05/University College
London**
University, UK. Designed
by The Partners
(AD: Jack Renwick;
D: Jess Philpott), 2005
A single identity binds
together a diverse
group of London
colleges. The portico
and dome belong to
William Wilkins's original
building for UCL.

06/Lands' End
Clothing and houseware
merchant, USA.
Designed by Pentagram
(D: DJ Stout), 2000
The name for this
catalogue and Internet
retailer of wholesome
outdoorsy clothes
originated when founder
Gary Comer started
a sailboat fittings
business in 1962. 'It
had a romantic ring
to it,' he wrote, 'and
conjured visions of a
point to depart from on
a perilous voyage.'

07/West Group
Legal research
services and online
information, USA.
Designed by Chermayeff
& Geismar Inc. (D: Steff
Geissbuhler) 1999

08/North Abbey
Strategic marketing
consultancy, UK.
Designed by Purpose,
2004

09/Stonehenge
Masterplan
development initiative,
UK. Designed by Atelier
Works and Alan Kitching,
2000
English Heritage,
the historic buildings
conservation agency,
has a long-term plan to
return Stonehenge to
a peaceful heathland
environment. The
typography was created
with the aid of master
letterpress typographer
Alan Kitching.

01/

02/

03/

04/

05/

06/

07/

08/

09/

10/

THE HEPWORTH **WAKEFIELD**

11/

01/Heyman Properties
Commercial property developer, USA. Designed by Chermayeff & Geismar Inc. (D: Henricus Kusbiantoro), 1997

02/Lowell Historic Board
Historic preservation agency, USA. Designed by Open, 1998
LHB is leading a programme of urban renewal in Lowell, Massachusetts, through the rehabilitation and re-use of the city's historic buildings. The logo depicts a new dawn for Lowell's old textile mills that once formed the city's economic and physical heart.

03/Ryan Associates
Construction contractor, USA. Designed by Elixir Design, 2002
An identity that conveys a commitment to design and collaboration with architects – unusual qualities in a contractor.

04/Escape Studios
Computer generated special effects school, UK. Designed by Bob Sakoui, 2004

05/Gotham Books
Publishing imprint, USA. Designed by Eric Baker Design (CD, D: Eric Baker; D: Eric Strohl), 2003
Books become building blocks for a New York – or Gotham – skyscraper.

06/The Furnace
Advertising agency, Australia. Designed by Frost Design (D: Vince Frost, Anthony Donovan)
The twin chimneys of the prone 'F' suggest a creative powerhouse.

07/Dupain
Rock band, France. Designed by Area 17, 1999
Echoes of Russian Revolutionary type and imagery appear in this logo for a band whose lyrics frequently deal with work conditions and factories.

08/The Skyscraper Museum
Not-for-profit museum, USA. Designed by Pentagram (D: Michael Gericke), 2001
The Skyscraper Museum in Battery Park City, Lower Manhattan, celebrates the architecture and skyline of the world's first vertical metropolis.

09/Exchange Place Center
Office development, USA. Designed by Lance Wyman, 1986
An identity that provides an appropriately postmodern view of Beyer Blinder Belle's elevations for the 30-storey Exchange Place Center in Jersey City.

10/Wentink Architekten
Architecture practice, The Netherlands. Designed by Studio Bau Winkel, 2004

11/The Hepworth
Art gallery, UK. Designed by Atelier Works, 2006
Reflected in the River Calder, the ice cool forms of this new gallery in Wakefield, West Yorkshire, by David Chipperfield Architects, make an 'H'.

01/

02/

03/

London Transport
Museum

04/

05/

06/

07/

 Berlin Airports

 HYDRO

 AutoRestore

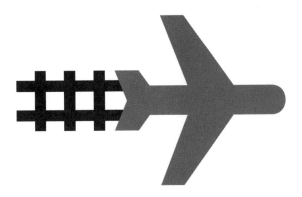

01/Carminal
Second-hand car dealership, Japan. Designed by Bravis International, 2006

02/NASA
Space agency, USA. Designed by James Modarelli, 1959
The original NASA 'meatball' logo, designed by a senior staff member of the agency's Lewis Research Center, was retired in 1975 in favour of the 'worm' logotype. In 1992, the meatball was revived to show that 'the magic is back at NASA'. But, as graphics managers have found, nostalgia has a price: the 1959 meatball, designed for a purely photographic printing

process, does not print well on laser printers and cannot be used at small sizes.

03/Individual Solutions
Car customization workshop, Germany. Designed by Pentagram (D: Justus Oehler, Uta Tjaden), 2006

04/London Transport Museum
Museum of public transport, UK. Designed by Minale Tattersfield, 1994
Bus and underground-rail culture, past and present, can be found at the London Transport Museum in Covent Garden, London.

05/Operation Seneca
Public transport crime-prevention campaign, UK. Designed by Crescent Lodge, 2001
Lucius Annaeus Seneca was a Roman philosopher and statesman who tried to solve the problems of his city's disaffected youth. A joint initiative by the Metropolitan Police and London's bus companies, Operation Seneca is intended to cut crime on public transport. A double-decker bus provides a strong, reassuring presence.

06/Sharemyride.co.uk
Car sharing scheme, UK. Designed by Coast Design (Sydney), 2005
Inspired by The Flintstones, whose cars didn't need any petrol.

07/New Bedford Whaling Museum
Museum of whaling history, USA. Designed by Malcolm Grear Designers, 1999

08/Berlin Airports
City airports group, Germany. Designed 2006
Berlin Airports (Berliner Flüghafen) is the umbrella brand for the city's three airports: Berlin-Tegel International, Tempelhof International and Berlin-Schönefeld International.

Rebranding marked the approval of major modernization and expansion plans in 2006.

09/Norsk Hydro
Oil, energy and aluminium group, Norway. Designed by Siegel & Gale, 2003
Introduced in 1910, the image of a Viking ship has become progressively more abstract over the years. The sail of three stripes first appeared on Leif Anisdal's logo in 1972.

10/AutoRestore
Car body repair shop chain, UK. Designed by Rose, 2005

11/Airtrain
Airport rail link, USA. Designed by Pentagram (D: Michael Gericke), 1998
Airtrain is the first rail service to New York's John F Kennedy International Airport. Its identity speaks to all travellers, whatever their language.

Van & Truck

LandMark

Sydney Car Market™
The Real Deal

13/ .... 14/ .... 15/ ....

16/ ....

12/Thielen
Winemaker, Germany
Designed by Together Design (D: Heidi Lightfoot, Katja Thielen, Jeff Fisher), 2004
The vast majority of modern corporate symbols are honed to a perceived perfection on computer screens. Too often, ideas are drained of humour and humanity by teams of marketing executives in search of a safe solution. The award-winning identity scheme for Thielen, a small private German wine label, is the opposite. Its simple one-colour illustration and handwritten typography share an almost homemade quality. This has nothing to do with the fact that its designer, Katja Thielen, is the daughter of the label's founder. Rather, it is a deliberate ploy to preserve the label's reputation as a well-kept secret that is spread by word-of-mouth, as it attempts to take on New World wines in the UK market. Other illustrations and some entertaining copywriting extend the branding across a website and packaging. The identity is fresh and free of cynicism, speaking directly of the honest artisanal qualities of a family-run wine business. It is not such a well-kept secret anymore: UK sales are exceeding targets. It helps when your dad is the client, but even so room exists for the chance imperfections of the hand-drawn in corporate identity.

13/Van & Truck
Nissan light commercial vehicle division, Japan. Designed by Bravis International, 2006

14/LandMark
Agricultural and hardware store chain, South Africa. Designed by Enterprise IG Africa (D: Dave Holland), 2006

15/Sydney Car Market
Second-hand car market, Australia. Designed by Coast Design (Sydney), 2004

16/King Abdul Aziz International Airport
International airport, Saudi Arabia. Designed by Wyman & Cannan (D: Lance Wyman, Farid Iskander, Ilham), 1977

01/

02/

03/

children's food education
FOUNDATION

Staffordshire

Unilever

01/National Parks of New York Harbor
Visitor destinations, USA. Designed by Chermayeff & Geismar Inc. (D: Steff Geissbuhler, Sagi Haviv), 2005
To raise awareness about the wealth of national parks and destinations around New York City, a family of wordmarks with embedded icons was developed to identify each of the sites as well as the umbrella brand itself.

02/Think London
Inward investment campaign, UK. Designed by Johnson Banks, 2003
When it comes to informing overseas businesses about London's selling points, 44 symbols – buildings and the rest – do the job better than one.

03/Lago di Garda
Tourist destination, Italy. Designed by Minale Tattersfield, 2005
This logo for a destination branding campaign marks a politically significant moment in Italian tourism: the coming together of the three regions previously competing for Lake Garda's tourist revenue – Trentino, Lombardy and Veneto.

04/Children's Food Education Foundation
Food awareness initiative, Australia. Designed by Coast Design (Sydney), 2004
This foundation highlights how much there is for little ones to learn – and enjoy – about what they eat, from the supermarket trolley to a place in a child's heart.

05/Staffordshire
Tourist destination, UK. Designed by Dragon Brands, 2006
To promote Staffordshire, centre of the UK ceramics industry, as a visitor destination with wider appeal, this mark paints the county as 'a world of possibilities'.

06/Arthaus Filmtheater Stuttgart
Cinema, Germany. Designed by Büro Uebele Visuelle Kommunikation, 2002
A picture puzzle whose elements – stars, letters and symbols – are playfully re-used in other applications.

07/Unilever
Consumer goods group, UK. Designed by Wolff Olins, 2004
A fundamental departure from Unilever's former identity as a stylized 'U', which had been in use since 1970, the latest brand supports the group's new mission: 'to add vitality to life'. The logo 'tells the story of Unilever and vitality', claimed the company at its launch. It comprises 25 icon-like illustrations representing Unilever and its brands: a spoon stands for cooking, a shirt symbolizes fresh laundry, a bee suggests hard work and biodiversity, and so on.

01/

02/

03/

CRICKET
AUSTRALIA

04/

05/

06/

07/

01/Dover Harbour Board and Port of Dover
Port authority, UK.
Designed by Minale
Tattersfield, 1987
Obliged to incorporate
the original port crest
into the new identity,
Minale Tattersfield
created a maritime-
style flag whose colours
– green and blue –
suggest the grass-
topped white cliffs of
Dover.

02/Alfa Romeo
Car manufacturer, Italy.
Designed by Romano
Cattaneo and Giuseppe
Merosi, 1910; updated
by Robilant & Associati,
1992
Given the job of
designing a badge
for the new ALFA
(Anonima Lombarda
Fabbrica Automobili)
car company, the young
draughtsman Cattaneo
spotted the serpent of
the Visconti family coat
of arms on the Filarete
Tower while waiting for a
tram in Piazza Castello.
With the help of Merosi,
he incorporated the
serpent and the red
cross of Milan into
a circle.

03/Cannes Party
Festival event, The
Netherlands. Designed
by The Stone Twins, 2003
This crest is for an
annual party at the
Cannes Advertising
Festival, hosted by
two Dutch/British
companies, Condor
Post Production and
Massive Music.

04/Bluestar Jets
Private jet charter
service, USA. Designed
by G2 Branding &
Design, 2005

05/Cricket Australia
Governing body for
cricket, Australia.
Designed by
FutureBrand Melbourne,
2005

**06/University of Chicago
Graduate School of
Business**
Business school, USA.
Designed by Crosby
Associates, 1999

07/BMW
Car manufacturer,
Germany. Designed 1917
The BMW badge has its
origins in World War I,
when the Bavarian
Luftwaffe planes
were painted in the
blue and white of the
Bayern coat of arms.
Bayerische Motoren
Werke manufactured the
aircraft's engines, and
the symbol developed
into a stylized propeller
in blue and white
segments. In 1929,
it appeared on the
company's first car.

British Embassy
Paris

09/

10/

11/

 Union Pacific Corporation

12/

08/UPS
Package delivery, transportation and logistics group, USA
Designed by FutureBrand, 2003
It had some design watchers – and many customers – fuming for months. UPS dropped its much-loved Paul Rand–designed parcel and shield in 2003, hoping to show that it was about more than delivering packages. The gift-like parcel and bow were replaced with an asymmetric sweep that, according to FutureBrand, 'expresses the evolution of the company's services and its commitment to leading the future of global commerce'. Many, however, simply see a swoosh where a heart-warming symbol used to be. The former logo's transparency has been replaced with a more tangible 3D form to make the mark a more integral part of UPS's distinctive brown delivery vehicles. The beefier appearance also suggests security. Expansion and growth demanded a change of identity, and customers might now be developing a different view of UPS. Whether this logo will get close to the 42 years that Rand's design lasted, only time will tell. What is certain is that the episode is proof of the strong bond that people sometimes forge with symbols, and how changes in identity can rouse passionate protest.

09/Amstel Gooi Vecht Hoogheemraadschap
Regional water management company, The Netherlands.
Designed by Total Identity, 1998

10/Foreign & Commonwealth Office
Government department for overseas relations and foreign affairs, UK. Designed by Moon Communications (D: Richard Moon), 1990
An update to the existing coat of arms to correct heraldic details and to ensure good reproduction at all sizes. The crest is used at every British embassy around the world.

11/Greenland Home Rule
National government, Greenland. Designed by Bysted, 2004
The image of a silver polar bear on a blue shield represented Greenland in the Danish coat of arms in the 17th century, but was not widely used by the country as a symbol until the 20th century.

12/Union Pacific Corporation
Transport, utilities and property corporation, USA. Designed by Chermayeff & Geismar Inc. (D: Steff Geissbuhler), 1981
The 1881 Trademark Act made businesses in America take their corporate identifiers a lot more seriously. Symbols became simpler and bolder, influenced by the current taste for Art Nouveau. The first Union Pacific shield with patriotic colours dates from that period. It was progressively simplified as the railroad grew into a corporation.

Families and sequences

The final section consists of just a single category, one that has emerged recently and has added a new dimension to identity design.

There is a degree of flexibility in most corporate identity systems: alternative configurations of logotype and symbol, for example, are often available for use in different applications and sizes. But, traditionally, those elements do not change. Many organizations today, though, particularly in creative and cultural fields, feel that a single set-in-stone symbol or logotype is too restrictive. Logos that evolve over time or across different applications, or that change, chameleon-like, to reflect new contexts offer a valuable means of keeping a demanding audience engaged. They suggest a restless, inquisitive and dynamic organization that promotes diversity and is at ease challenging perceptions of itself. And that is the kind of image that many art galleries, restaurants, publishers and creative consultancies would like to project.

It is a postmodern pluralist approach to identity that can be traced back to the Memphis design movement of the early 1980s. Memphis was a reaction to rational system-based design of the 1970s, an outburst of texture, colour, pattern and form. One logo would never be enough for Memphis: Christoph Radl and Valentina Grego created an entire series of brash blocky logotype designs that stuck a tongue out at the prevailing wisdom of identifying companies with just one highly polished, heavily policed logo.

Owners of today's logo families and sequences are not operating under the same agenda. They are merely making the most of advances in design and printing technology, which have brought the freedom to produce variations on a theme to suit different applications. On websites, identities can be brought to life in mini animations, which has led designers to experiment with sequential series of logos in more traditional media. Diversity, dynamism and creativity are attributes that more mainstream organizations than those represented here are trying to claim as their own. It is likely that the kind of mobile mutating identities seen on the following pages will become the norm in the years to come.

Heide
Museum of
Modern Art
Heide

Heide
Museum of
Modern Art
Heide

Heide
Museum of
Modern Art
Heide

Heide
Museum of
Modern Art
Heide

Heide
Museum of
Modern Art
Heide

Heide
Museum of
Modern Art
Heide

Heide
Museum of
Modern Art
Heide

Heide
Museum of
Modern Art
Heide

Heide
Museum of
Modern Art
Heide

Heide
Museum of
Modern Art
Heide

Heide
Museum of
Modern Art
Heide

Heide
Museum of
Modern Art
Heide

Heide
Museum of
Modern Art
Heide

Heide
Museum of
Modern Art
Heide

Heide
Museum of
Modern Art
Heide

Heide
Museum of
Modern Art
Heide

Heide
Museum of
Modern Art
Heide

Heide
Museum of
Modern Art
Heide

Heide
Museum of
Modern Art
Heide

Heide
Museum of
Modern Art
Heide

Heide
Museum of
Modern Art
Heide

Heide
Museum of
Modern Art
Heide

Heide
Museum of
Modern Art
Heide

Heide
Museum of
Modern Art
Heide

Heide
Museum of
Modern Art
Heide

Heide
Museum of
Modern Art
Heide

Heide
Museum of
Modern Art
Heide

Heide
Museum of
Modern Art
Heide

Heide
Museum of
Modern Art
Heide

Heide
Museum of
Modern Art
Heide

Heide
Museum of
Modern Art
Heide

Heide
Museum of
Modern Art
Heide

Heide
Museum of
Modern Art
Heide

Heide
Museum of
Modern Art
Heide

Heide
Museum of
Modern Art
Heide

Heide
Museum of
Modern Art
Heide

Heide
Museum of
Modern Art
Heide

Heide
Museum of
Modern Art
Heide

Heide
Museum of
Modern Art
Heide

Heide
Museum of
Modern Art
Heide

Heide
Museum of
Modern Art
Heide

Heide
Museum of
Modern Art
Heide

Heide
Museum of
Modern Art
Heide

Heide
Museum of
Modern Art
Heide

Heide
Museum of
Modern Art
Heide

Heide
Museum of
Modern Art
Heide

Heide
Museum of
Modern Art
Heide

Heide
Museum of
Modern Art
Heide

Heide
Museum of
Modern Art
Heide

Heide
Museum of
Modern Art
Heide

01/Heide Museum of Modern Art
Public art museum, Australia. Designed by GollingsPidgeon
Heide is an unusual space, combining indoor and outdoor environments and traditional and contemporary art and design. Its identity is a reflection of this diversity. The layout, colour and Heide script are constants, providing continuity and consistency, but the typography changes to offer a new and appropriate identity for each exhibition.

02/TNN
Cable TV network, USA. Designed by Segura Inc, 2005
Three from a series of logo variations designed for a channel keen to distance itself from its country and western music origins.

03/Little, Brown Book Group
Publishing house, UK. Designed by Unreal, 2006
Objects that are little and brown represent the attributes of the rebranded Time Warner Book Group.

3.0 Families and sequences

04/De Lindenhof
Restaurant, The
Netherlands. Designed
by ankerxstrijbos, 2006
A system of logos,
designed to be used
individually or in
groups, represents
De Lindenhof, a two
Michelin star restaurant
in the Dutch countryside.

**05/Holborn Business
Partnership**
Destination branding
initiative, UK. Designed
by CDT, 2006
The district of Holborn,
in what is fashionably
called London's
'Midtown', lies between
the capital's historic
commercial and
administrative centres
(the City of London
and Westminster).
But, it has a compelling
history of its own, as the
heartland of London's
publishing and legal
traditions. Being so well
placed and as home
to service industries
and numerous green
squares, the area has
a lot to offer business.
CDT devised an identity
system for the Holborn
Business Partnership to

capture the diversity of
the area, using banners
hung from lamp posts
and a logotype that
can be easily tailored
to different campaigns.

**06/Vrijheidsfestival
Den Haag**
'Liberty' festival, The
Netherlands. Designed
by NLXL, 2005
Liberty festivals are
held annually in
towns throughout
The Netherlands to
commemorate the end
of World War II. This
flexible identity system
reflects the unusual
level of diversity in
The Hague's festival
programme, which
includes events and
performances for
people of all ages.

07/100% Proof
Editing and
proofreading service,
UK. Designed by
Sarah Tripp, 2005
100% Proof specializes
in editing and
proofreading artists'
books, catalogues and
journals. A discussion
about the relationship
between writing and
design, and the aim
that the two disciplines
share of maximizing
the readability of text,
led to the identity.
Disembodied serifs
and ligatures – devices
usually used to enhance
legibility – were the
starting points for a
sequence of marks that
grow like tendrils across
the page to represent
the firm's investment of
its profits in new work.

08/Oni
Japanese restaurant,
The Netherlands.
Designed by NLXL, 2004
This Japanese
restaurant in The Hague
specializes in the
art of the bento box,
which involves creating
aesthetically pleasing
arrangements out of
bite-size helpings of
fish or meat, rice and
vegetables. The multiple
logos do the same
with the letterforms of
the restaurant's name,
creating a series of
animated humanistic
variations.

**09/The Henry Lydiate
Partnership**
Creative arts business
consultancy, UK.
Designed by Thomas
Manss & Company, 2006
Based on the endless
visual permutations of
a kaleidoscope, this
identity portrays the
four partners as offering
arts and cultural
clients an imaginative,
non-formulaic, client-
centred type of business
consultancy.

fresh.

fresh.

fresh.

cccCC

10/1508
Graphic design studio, Denmark. Designed by A2/SW/HK, 2001
The Dymaxion map of earth, created by the visionary Buckminster Fuller, gave a more accurate representation of the relative size of land masses than had been seen before in two dimensions. Previous maps, in attempting to transform the 3D globe into a flat rectangle, had exaggerated the size of land masses near the poles. Fuller projected a globe onto an icosahedron (a volume with 20 triangular sides), which could then be unfolded and flattened in numerous different ways. A2/SW/HK's award-winning identity

for Danish design group 1508 uses the Dymaxion projection as a template for a logo that shifts formation across media, mutating each time it appears on a different team member's business card.

11/Fresh
Professional development services for the legal industry, UK. Designed by Sarah Tripp, 2004
In response to a brief calling for an identity that alludes to change, development and a bespoke client-focused approach, this identity comprises a series of 'particle explosions' that feature, one each, on different applications.

12/Cubitt Artists
Artists' studios, UK. Designed by A2/SW/HK, 2001
Alternative letterpress 'C's represent this artists' community, following its move to a former printer's workshop in Islington, north London.

Dictionary of
Australian Artists
Online.

Dictionary of
Australian Artists
Online.

Dictionary of
Australian Artists
Online.

Dictionary of
Australian Artists
Online.

Dictionary of
Australian Artists
Online.

Dictionary of
Australian Artists
Online.

Dictionary of
Australian Artists
Online.

Dictionary of
Australian Artists
Online.

Dictionary of
Australian Artists
Online.

Dictionary of
Australian Artists
Online.

Dictionary of
Australian Artists
Online.

Dictionary of
Australian Artists
Online.

Dictionary of
Australian Artists
Online.

Dictionary of
Australian Artists
Online.

Dictionary of
Australian Artists
Online.

Dictionary of
Australian Artists
Online.

13/Dictionary of Australian Artists Online
Web-based search tool, Australia. Designed by Naughtyfish, 2005
The DAAO provides access to information and biographical data from Australia's major universities and art galleries. Taking the dictionary's A to Z as a starting point, the logo consists of 26 coloured pixels, each representing a letter of the alphabet, which are dynamically rearranged to create a number of alternative images suited to different types of communication.

14/Roppongi Hills
Property development, Japan. Designed by Barnbrook Design, 2003
Roppongi Hills may sound rural but is, in fact, one of the largest urban integrated property developments in the world. Built by the tycoon Minoru Mori, the £4-billion Tokyo mega complex includes office space, apartments, shops, restaurants, cinemas, a hotel, a museum and several parks. The identity for the complex refers, though, to the site's rustic past. The kanji characters for 'Roppongi' mean 'six trees', and make a connection with the name 'mori', which translates as 'forest'.

The 'six trees' were reduced to six circles, providing the basis for a series of logotypes in different fonts, as well as operating as a logo in their own right.

15/Urban Age Conferences
Conference programme, UK. Designed by Atelier Works, 2005
A collection of Victor Vasarely-inspired architectural planes identify Urban Age, a two-year series of international conferences held around the world by a network of universities eminent in the field of urban studies.

3.0 Families and
sequences

16/Standard 8
Manufacturer of
furniture and exhibition
systems, UK. Designed
by Browns, 2005
Eight different fleurons,
each made up of a
figure 8 in a different
font and repeated eight
times, demonstrate the
extraordinary variety
and elegance possible
from relatively simple
components, thereby
capturing Standard
8's skill at design
and construction.

17/Glacis Beisl
Restaurant, Austria.
Designed by Büro X
(AD: Andreas Miedaner;
D: Veronika Neubauer),
2006
One of Vienna's
culinary landmarks,
Glacis Beisl is an old-
fashioned outdoor
tavern of the kind
that, traditionally, did
not have a consistent
visual identity or logo.
Sign painters, printers
and, later, neon sign
makers simply made
their own selection of
typeface from what they
had available, which
led eventually to each
establishment boasting
a profusion of logos.
When Glacis Beisl
re-opened after a
major update in 2006,
its new identity

comprised a trio of
wordmarks whose
knowing gaucheness
recalls more innocent
times.

18/Village Twin
Independent cinema,
Australia. Designed
by Inkahoots, 2005.
The changing neo-
psychedelic decoration
that frames the heart
and twin 'V's references
the two-screen cinema's
late 1960s to early 1970s
architecture.

crossroads for ideas

crossroads for ideas

crossroads for ideas

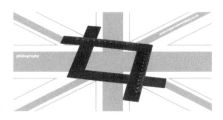

crossroads for ideas

De Stromen   Boekholt   Meerweide

19/Crossroads for Ideas
Diplomatic campaign,
UK. Designed by HGV
(D: Tony Muranita,
Piers Carter), 2004
This campaign by
the British Council
and The Foreign and
Commonwealth Office
seeks to bring together
talented young people
from the UK and the
eight central European
states that joined the
EU in May 2004. The
reversed colours of the
Union flag depict an
intersection of eight
paths where ideas,
experience and skills
can be exchanged.

20/De Stromen
Senior citizens'
care provider, The
Netherlands. Designed
by Total Identity
(D: Jeanette Kaptein),
1997

21/Mesh
Digital media agency,
UK. Designed by Blast,
2004
A company with four
main areas of business
has a multilayered
identity.

Client index

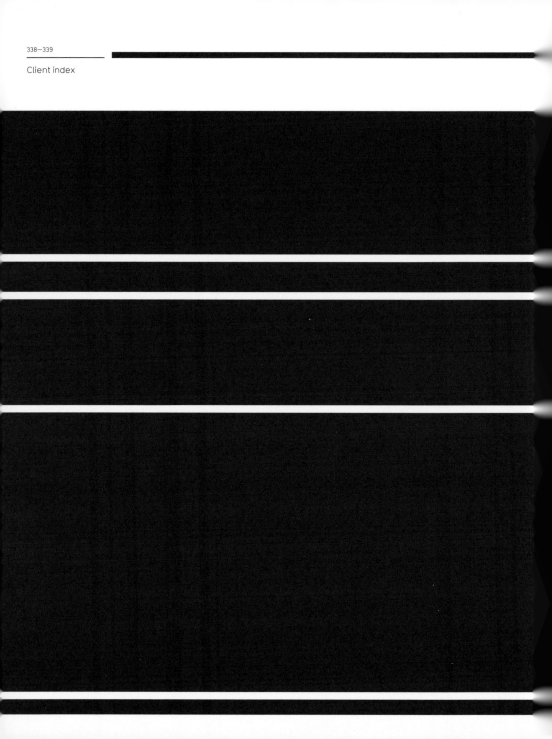

Client index

Designer index

Credits.
Photography
Page 17
Whitechapel Art Gallery,
Andrew G. Hobbs